THE PELICAN SHAKESPEARE
GENERAL EDITORS

STEPHEN ORGEL
A. R. BRAUNMULLER

The Tragedy of King Richard the Second

William Macready (1793–1873) as Richard II at the
Haymarket Theatre in 1850, one of his last roles before
his retirement in 1851. The production was praised
for its unusual fidelity to Shakespeare's text and
for the historical accuracy of its decor.

William Shakespeare

The Tragedy of
King Richard the Second

EDITED BY FRANCES E. DOLAN

PENGUIN BOOKS

PENGUIN BOOKS

Published by the Penguin Group

Penguin Group (USA) Inc., 375 Hudson Street, New York, New York 10014, U.S.A.
Penguin Group (Canada), 90 Eglinton Avenue East, Suite 700, Toronto,
Ontario, Canada M4P 2Y3 (a division of Pearson Penguin Canada Inc.)
Penguin Books Ltd, 80 Strand, London WC2R 0RL, England
Penguin Ireland, 25 St Stephen's Green, Dublin 2, Ireland (a division of Penguin Books Ltd)
Penguin Group (Australia), 250 Camberwell Road, Camberwell,
Victoria 3124, Australia (a division of Pearson Australia Group Pty Ltd)
Penguin Books India Pvt Ltd, 11 Community Centre, Panchsheel Park, New Delhi – 110 017, India
Penguin Group (NZ), 67 Apollo Drive, Rosedale, North Shore 0632, New Zealand
(a division of Pearson New Zealand Ltd)
Penguin Books (South Africa) (Pty) Ltd, 24 Sturdee Avenue,
Rosebank, Johannesburg 2196, South Africa

Penguin Books Ltd, Registered Offices: 80 Strand, London WC2R 0RL, England

The Tragedy of King Richard the Second edited
by Matthew W. Black published in the
United States of America in Penguin Books 1957
Revised edition published 1970
This new edition edited by Frances E. Dolan published 2000

20

Copyright © Penguin Books Inc., 1957, 1970
Copyright © Penguin Putnam Inc., 2000
All rights reserved

ISBN 978-0-14-071482-1
(CIP data available)

Printed in the United States of America
Set in Adobe Garamond
Designed by Virginia Norey

Contents

Publisher's Note

IT IS ALMOST half a century since the first volumes of the Pelican Shakespeare appeared under the general editorship of Alfred Harbage. The fact that a new edition, rather than simply a revision, has been undertaken reflects the profound changes textual and critical studies of Shakespeare have undergone in the past twenty years. For the new Pelican series, the texts of the plays and poems have been thoroughly revised in accordance with recent scholarship, and in some cases have been entirely reedited. New introductions and notes have been provided in all the volumes. But the new Shakespeare is also designed as a successor to the original series; the previous editions have been taken into account, and the advice of the previous editors has been solicited where it was feasible to do so.

Certain textual features of the new Pelican Shakespeare should be particularly noted. All lines are numbered that contain a word, phrase, or allusion explained in the glossarial notes. In addition, for convenience, every tenth line is also numbered, in italics when no annotation is indicated. The intrusive and often inaccurate place headings inserted by early editors are omitted (as is becoming standard practice), but for the convenience of those who miss them, an indication of locale now appears as the first item in the annotation of each scene.

In the interest of both elegance and utility, each speech prefix is set in a separate line when the speaker's lines are in verse, except when those words form the second half of a verse line. Thus the verse form of the speech is kept visually intact. What is printed as verse and what is printed as prose has, in general, the authority of the original texts. Departures from the original texts in this regard have only the authority of editorial tradition and the judgment of the Pelican editors; and, in a few instances, are admittedly arbitrary.

The Theatrical World

Economic realities determined the theatrical world in which Shakespeare's plays were written, performed, and received. For centuries in England, the primary theatrical tradition was nonprofessional. Craft guilds (or "mysteries") provided religious drama – mystery plays – as part of the celebration of religious and civic festivals, and schools and universities staged classical and neoclassical drama in both Latin and English as part of their curricula. In these forms, drama was established and socially acceptable. Professional theater, in contrast, existed on the margins of society. The acting companies were itinerant; playhouses could be any available space – the great halls of the aristocracy, town squares, civic halls, inn yards, fair booths, or open fields – and income was sporadic, dependent on the passing of the hat or on the bounty of local patrons. The actors, moreover, were considered little better than vagabonds, constantly in danger of arrest or expulsion.

In the late 1560s and 1570s, however, English professional theater began to gain respectability. Wealthy aristocrats fond of drama – the Lord Admiral, for example, or the Lord Chamberlain – took acting companies under their protection so that the players technically became members of their households and were no longer subject to arrest as homeless or masterless men. Permanent theaters were first built at this time as well, allowing the companies to control and charge for entry to their performances.

Shakespeare's livelihood, and the stunning artistic explosion in which he participated, depended on pragmatic and architectural effort. Professional theater requires ways to restrict access to its offerings; if it does not, and admission fees cannot be charged, the actors do not get paid, the costumes go to a pawnbroker, and there is no such thing as a professional, ongoing theatrical tradition. The answer to that economic need arrived in the late 1560s and 1570s with the creation of the so-called public or amphitheater playhouse. Recent discoveries indicate that the precursor of the Globe playhouse in London (where Shakespeare's mature plays were presented) and the Rose theater (which presented Christopher Marlowe's plays and some of Shakespeare's earliest ones) was the Red Lion theater of 1567. Archaeological studies of the foundations of the Rose and Globe theaters have revealed that the open-air theater of the 1590s and later was probably a polygonal building with fourteen to twenty or twenty-four sides, multistoried, from 75 to 100 feet in diameter, with a raised, partly covered "thrust" stage that projected into a group of standing patrons, or "groundlings," and a covered gallery, seating up to 2,500 or more (very crowded) spectators.

These theaters might have been about half full on any given day, though the audiences were larger on holidays or when a play was advertised, as old and new were, through printed playbills posted around London. The metropolitan area's late-Tudor, early-Stuart population (circa 1590-1620) has been estimated at about 150,000 to 250,000. It has been supposed that in the mid-1590s there were about 15,000 spectators per week at the public theaters; thus, as many as 10 percent of the local population went to the theater regularly. Consequently, the theaters' repertories – the plays available for this experienced and frequent audience – had to change often: in the month between September 15 and October 15, 1595, for instance, the Lord Admiral's Men performed twenty-eight times in eighteen different plays.

Since natural light illuminated the amphitheaters' stages, performances began between noon and two o'clock and ran without a break for two or three hours. They often concluded with a jig, a fencing display, or some other nondramatic exhibition. Weather conditions determined the season for the amphitheaters: plays were performed every day (including Sundays, sometimes, to clerical dismay) except during Lent – the forty days before Easter – or periods of plague, or sometimes during the summer months when law courts were not in session and the most affluent members of the audience were not in London.

To a modern theatergoer, an amphitheater stage like that of the Rose or Globe would appear an unfamiliar mixture of plainness and elaborate decoration. Much of the structure was carved or painted, sometimes to imitate marble; elsewhere, as under the canopy projecting over the stage, to represent the stars and the zodiac. Appropriate painted canvas pictures (of Jerusalem, for example, if the play was set in that city) were apparently hung on the wall behind the acting area, and tragedies were accompanied by black hangings, presumably something like crepe festoons or bunting. Although these theaters did not employ what we would call scenery, early modern spectators saw numerous large props, such as the "bar" at which a prisoner stood during a trial, the "mossy bank" where lovers reclined, an arbor for amorous conversation, a chariot, gallows, tables, trees, beds, thrones, writing desks, and so forth. Audiences might learn a scene's location from a sign (reading "Athens," for example) carried across the stage (as in Bertolt Brecht's twentieth-century productions). Equally captivating (and equally irritating to the theater's enemies) were the rich costumes and personal props the actors used: the most valuable items in the surviving theatrical inventories are the swords, gowns, robes, crowns, and other items worn or carried by the performers.

Magic appealed to Shakespeare's audiences as much as it does to us today, and the theater exploited many deceptive and spectacular devices. A winch in the loft above the stage, called "the heavens," could lower and raise actors playing gods, goddesses, and other supernatural figures to and from the main acting area, just as one or more trapdoors permitted entrances and exits to and from the area, called "hell," beneath the stage. Actors wore elementary makeup such as wigs, false beards, and face paint, and they employed pig's bladders filled with animal blood to make wounds seem more real. They had rudimentary but effective ways of pretending to behead or hang a person. Supernumeraries (stagehands or actors not needed in a particular scene) could make thunder sounds (by shaking a metal sheet or rolling an iron ball down a chute) and show lightning (by blowing inflammable resin through tubes into a flame). Elaborate fireworks enhanced the effects of dragons flying through the air or imitated such celestial phenomena as comets, shooting stars, and multiple suns. Horses' hoofbeats, bells (located perhaps in the tower above the stage), trumpets and drums, clocks, cannon shots and gunshots, and the like were common sound effects. And the music of viols, cornets, oboes, and recorders was a regular feature of theatrical performances.

For two relatively brief spans, from the late 1570s to 1590 and from 1599 to 1614, the amphitheaters competed with the so-called private, or indoor, theaters, which originated as, or later represented themselves as, educational institutions training boys as singers for church services and court performances. These indoor theaters had two features that were distinct from the amphitheaters': their personnel and their playing spaces. The amphitheaters' adult companies included both adult men, who played the male roles, and boys, who played the female roles; the private, or indoor, theater companies, on the other hand, were entirely composed of boys aged about 8 to 16, who were, or could pretend to be, candidates for singers in a church or a royal boys' choir. (Until 1660, professional theatrical companies included no women.) The playing space would appear much more familiar to modern audiences than the long-vanished amphitheaters; the later indoor theaters were, in fact, the ancestors of the typical modern theater. They were enclosed spaces, usually rectangular, with the stage filling one end of the rectangle and the audience arrayed in seats or benches across (and sometimes lining) the building's longer axis. These spaces staged plays less frequently than the public theaters (perhaps only once a week) and held far fewer spectators than the amphitheaters: about 200 to 600, as opposed to 2,500 or more. Fewer patrons mean a smaller gross income, unless each pays more. Not surprisingly, then, private theaters charged higher prices than the amphitheaters, probably sixpence, as opposed to a penny for the cheapest entry.

Protected from the weather, the indoor theaters presented plays later in the day than the amphitheaters, and used artificial illumination – candles in sconces or candelabra. But candles melt, and need replacing, snuffing, and trimming, and these practical requirements may have been part of the reason the indoor theaters introduced breaks in the performance, the intermission so dear to the heart of theatergoers and to the pocketbooks of theater concessionaires ever since. Whether motivated by the need to tend to the candles or by the entrepreneurs' wishing to sell oranges and liquor, or both, the indoor theaters eventually established the modern convention of the non-continuous performance. In the early modern "private" theater, musical performances apparently filled the intermissions, which in Stuart theater jargon seem to have been called "acts."

At the end of the first decade of the seventeenth century, the distinction between public amphitheaters and private indoor companies ceased. For various cultural, political, and economic reasons, individual companies gained control of both the public, open-air theaters and the indoor ones, and companies mixing adult men and boys took over the formerly "private" theaters. Despite the death of the boys' companies and of their highly innovative theaters (for which such luminous playwrights as Ben Jonson, George Chapman, and John Marston wrote), their playing spaces and conventions had an immense impact on subsequent plays: not merely for the intervals (which stressed the artistic and architectonic importance of "acts"), but also because they introduced political and social satire as a popular dramatic ingredient, even in tragedy, and a wider range of actorly effects, encouraged by their more intimate playing spaces.

Even the briefest sketch of the Shakespearean theatrical world would be incomplete without some comment on the social and cultural dimensions of theaters and playing in the period. In an intensely hierarchical and status-conscious society, professional actors and their ventures had hardly any respectability; as we have indicated, to protect themselves against laws designed to curb vagabondage and the increase of masterless men, actors resorted to the near-fiction that they were the servants of noble masters, and wore their distinctive livery. Hence the company for which Shakespeare wrote in the 1590s called itself the Lord Chamberlain's Men and pretended that the public, money-getting performances were in fact rehearsals for private performances before that high court official. From 1598, the Privy Council had licensed theatrical companies, and after 1603, with the accession of King James I, the companies gained explicit royal protection, just as the Queen's Men had for a time under Queen Elizabeth. The Chamberlain's Men became the King's Men, and the other companies were patronized by the other members of the royal family.

These designations were legal fictions that half-concealed an important economic and social development, the evolution away from the theater's organization on the model of the guild, a self-regulating confraternity of individual artisans, into a proto-capitalist organization. Shakespeare's company became a joint-stock company, where persons who supplied capital and, in some cases, such as Shakespeare's, capital and talent, employed themselves and others in earning a return on that capital. This development meant that actors and theater companies were outside both the traditional guild structures, which required some form of civic or royal charter, and the feudal household organization of master-and-servant. This anomalous, maverick social and economic condition made theater companies practically unruly and potentially even dangerous; consequently, numerous official bodies – including the London metropolitan and ecclesiastical authorities as well as, occasionally, the royal court itself – tried, without much success, to control and even to disband them.

Public officials had good reason to want to close the theaters: they were attractive nuisances – they drew often riotous crowds, they were always noisy, and they could be politically offensive and socially insubordinate. Until the Civil War, however, anti-theatrical forces failed to shut down professional theater, for many reasons – limited surveillance and few police powers, tensions or outright hostilities among the agencies that sought to check or channel theatrical activity, and lack of clear policies for control. Another reason must have been the theaters' undeniable popularity. Curtailing any activity enjoyed by such a substantial percentage of the population was difficult, as various Roman emperors attempting to limit circuses had learned, and the Tudor-Stuart audience was not merely large, it was socially diverse and included women. The prevalence of public entertainment in this period has been underestimated. In fact, fairs, holidays, games, sporting events, the equivalent of modern parades, freak shows, and street exhibitions all abounded, but the theater was the most widely and frequently available entertainment to which people of every class had access. That fact helps account both for its quantity and for the fear and anger it aroused.

WILLIAM SHAKESPEARE OF STRATFORD-UPON-AVON, GENTLEMAN

Many people have said that we know very little about William Shakespeare's life – pinheads and postcards are often mentioned as appropriately tiny surfaces on which to record the available information. More imaginatively and perhaps more correctly, Ralph Waldo Emerson wrote, "Shakespeare is the only biographer of Shakespeare. . . . So far from Shakespeare's being the least known, he is the one person in all modern history fully known to us."

In fact, we know more about Shakespeare's life than we do about almost any other English writer's of his era. His last will and testament (dated March 25, 1616) survives, as do numerous legal contracts and court documents involving Shakespeare as principal or witness, and parish records in Stratford and London. Shakespeare appears quite often in official records of King James's royal court, and of course Shakespeare's name appears on numerous title pages and in the written and recorded words of his literary contemporaries Robert Greene, Henry Chettle, Francis Meres, John Davies of Hereford, Ben Jonson, and many others. Indeed, if we make due allowance for the bloating of modern, run-of-the-mill bureaucratic records, more information has survived over the past four hundred years about William Shakespeare of Stratford-upon-Avon, Warwickshire, than is likely to survive in the next four hundred years about any reader of these words.

What we do not have are entire categories of information – Shakespeare's private letters or diaries, drafts and revisions of poems and plays, critical prefaces or essays, commendatory verse for other writers' works, or instructions guiding his fellow actors in their performances, for instance – that we imagine would help us understand and appreciate his surviving writings. For all we know, many such data never existed as written records. Many literary and theatrical critics, not knowing what might once have existed, more or less cheerfully accept the situation; some even make a theoretical virtue of it by claiming that such data are irrelevant to understanding and interpreting the plays and poems.

So, what do we know about William Shakespeare, the man responsible for thirty-seven or perhaps more plays, more than 150 sonnets, two lengthy narrative poems, and some shorter poems?

While many families by the name of Shakespeare (or some variant spelling) can be identified in the English Midlands as far back as the twelfth century, it seems likely that the dramatist's grandfather, Richard, moved to Snitterfield, a town not far from Stratford-upon-Avon, sometime before 1529. In Snitterfield, Richard Shakespeare leased farmland from the very wealthy Robert Arden. By 1552, Richard's son John had moved to a large house on Henley Street in Stratford-upon-Avon, the house that stands today as "The Birthplace." In Stratford, John Shakespeare traded as a glover, dealt in wool, and lent money at interest; he also served in a variety of civic posts, including "High Bailiff," the municipality's equivalent of mayor. In 1557, he married Robert Arden's youngest daughter, Mary. Mary and John had four sons – William was the oldest – and four daughters, of whom only Joan outlived her most celebrated sibling. William was baptized (an event entered in the Stratford parish church records) on April 26, 1564, and it has become customary, without any good factual support, to suppose he was born on April 23, which happens to be the feast day of Saint George, patron saint of England, and is also the date on which he died, in 1616. Shakespeare married Anne Hathaway in 1582, when he was eighteen and she was twenty-six; their first child was born five months later. It has been generally assumed that the marriage was enforced and subsequently unhappy, but these are only assumptions; it has been estimated, for instance, that up to one third of Elizabethan brides were pregnant when they married. Anne and William Shakespeare had three children: Susanna, who married a prominent local physician, John Hall; and the twins Hamnet, who died young in 1596, and Judith, who married Thomas Quiney – apparently a rather shady individual. The name Hamnet was unusual but not unique: he and his twin sister were named for their godparents, Shakespeare's neighbors Hamnet and Judith Sadler. Shakespeare's father died in 1601 (the year of *Hamlet*), and Mary Arden Shakespeare died in 1608 (the year of *Coriolanus*). William Shakespeare's last surviving direct descendant was his granddaughter Elizabeth Hall, who died in 1670.

Between the birth of the twins in 1585 and a dear reference to Shakespeare as a practicing London dramatist in Robert Greene's sensationalizing, satiric pamphlet, *Greene's Groatsworth of Wit* (1592), there is no record of where William Shakespeare was or what he was doing. These seven so-called lost years have been imaginatively filled by scholars and other students of Shakespeare: some think he traveled to Italy, or fought in the Low Countries, or studied law or medicine, or worked as an apprentice actor/writer, and so on to even more fanciful possibilities. Whatever the biographical facts for those "lost" years, Greene's nasty remarks in 1592 testify to professional envy and to the fact that Shakespeare already had a successful career in London. Speaking to his fellow playwrights, Greene warns both generally and specifically:

> . . . trust them [actors] not: for there is an upstart crow, beautified with our feathers, that with his tiger's heart wrapped in a player's hide supposes he is as well able to bombast out a blank verse as the best of you; and being an absolute Johannes Factotum, is in his own conceit the only Shake-scene in a country.

The passage mimics a line from *3 Henry VI* (hence the play must have been performed before Greene wrote) and seems to say that "Shake-scene" is both actor and playwright, a jack-of-all-trades. That same year, Henry Chettle protested Greene's remarks in *Kind-Heart's Dream,* and each of the next two years saw the publication of poems – *Venus and Adonis* and *The Rape of Lucrece,* respectively – publicly ascribed to (and dedicated by) Shakespeare. Early in 1595 he was named as one of the senior members of a prominent acting company, the Lord Chamberlain's Men, when they received payment for court performances during the 1594 Christmas season.

Clearly, Shakespeare had achieved both success and reputation in London. In 1596, upon Shakespeare's application, the College of Arms granted his father the now-familiar coat of arms he had taken the first steps to obtain almost twenty years before, and in 1598, John's son – now permitted to call himself "gentleman" – took a 10 percent share in the new Globe playhouse. In 1597, he bought a substantial bourgeois house, called New Place, in Stratford – the garden remains, but Shakespeare's house, several times rebuilt, was torn down in 1759 – and over the next few years Shakespeare spent large sums buying land and making other investments in the town and its environs. Though he worked in London, his family remained in Stratford, and he seems always to have considered Stratford the home he would eventually return to. Something approaching a disinterested appreciation of Shakespeare's popular and professional status appears in Francis Meres's *Palladis Tamia* (1598), a not especially imaginative and perhaps therefore persuasive record of literary reputations. Reviewing contemporary English writers, Meres lists the titles of many of Shakespeare's plays, including one not now known, *Love's Labor's Won,* and praises his "mellifluous & hony-tongued" "sugred Sonnets," which were then circulating in manuscript (they were first collected in 1609). Meres describes Shakespeare as "one of the best" English playwrights of both comedy and tragedy. In *Remains . . . Concerning Britain* (1605), William Camden – a more authoritative source than the imitative Meres – calls Shakespeare one of the "most pregnant witts of these our times" and joins him with such writers as Chapman, Daniel, Jonson, Marston, and Spenser. During the first decades of the seventeenth century, publishers began to attribute numerous play quartos, including some non-Shakespearean ones, to Shakespeare, either by name or initials, and we may assume that they deemed Shakespeare's name and supposed authorship, true or false, commercially attractive.

For the next ten years or so, various records show

Shakespeare's dual career as playwright and man of the theater in London, and as an important local figure in Stratford. In 1608-9 his acting company – designated the "King's Men" soon after King James had succeeded Queen Elizabeth in 1603 – rented, refurbished, and opened a small interior playing space, the Blackfriars theater, in London, and Shakespeare was once again listed as a substantial sharer in the group of proprietors of the playhouse. By May 11, 1612, however, he describes himself as a Stratford resident in a London lawsuit – an indication that he had withdrawn from day-to-day professional activity and returned to the town where he had always had his main financial interests. When Shakespeare bought a substantial residential building in London, the Blackfriars Gatehouse, close to the theater of the same name, on March 10, 1613, he is recorded as William Shakespeare "of Stratford upon Avon in the county of Warwick, gentleman," and he named several London residents as the building's trustees. Still, he continued to participate in theatrical activity: when the new Earl of Rutland needed an allegorical design to bear as a shield, or *impresa,* at the celebration of King James's Accession Day, March 24, 1613, the earl's accountant recorded a payment of 44 shillings to Shakespeare for the device with its motto.

For the last few years of his life, Shakespeare evidently concentrated his activities in the town of his birth. Most of the final records concern business transactions in Stratford, ending with the notation of his death on April 23, 1616, and burial in Holy Trinity Church, Stratford-upon-Avon.

THE QUESTION OF AUTHORSHIP

The history of ascribing Shakespeare's plays (the poems do not come up so often) to someone else began, as it continues, peculiarly. The earliest published claim that someone else wrote Shakespeare's plays appeared in an

1856 article by Delia Bacon in the American journal *Putnam's Monthly* – although an Englishman, Thomas Wilmot, had shared his doubts in private (even secretive) conversations with friends near the end of the eighteenth century. Bacon's was a sad personal history that ended in madness and poverty, but the year after her article, she published, with great difficulty and the bemused assistance of Nathaniel Hawthorne (then United States Consul in Liverpool, England), her *Philosophy of the Plays of Shakspere Unfolded.* This huge, ornately written, confusing farrago is almost unreadable; sometimes its intents, to say nothing of its arguments, disappear entirely beneath near-raving, ecstatic writing. Tumbled in with much supposed "philosophy" appear the claims that Francis Bacon (from whom Delia Bacon eventually claimed descent), Walter Ralegh, and several other contemporaries of Shakespeare's had written the plays. The book had little impact except as a ridiculed curiosity.

Once proposed, however, the issue gained momentum among people whose conviction was the greater in proportion to their ignorance of sixteenth- and seventeenth-century English literature, history, and society. Another American amateur, Catherine P. Ashmead Windle, made the next influential contribution to the cause when she published *Report to the British Museum* (1882), wherein she promised to open "the Cipher of Francis Bacon," though what she mostly offers, in the words of S. Schoenbaum, is "demented allegorizing." An entire new cottage industry grew from Windle's suggestion that the texts contain hidden, cryptographically discoverable ciphers – "clues" – to their authorship; and today there are not only books devoted to the putative ciphers, but also pamphlets, journals, and newsletters.

Although Baconians have led the pack of those seeking a substitute Shakespeare, in *"Shakespeare" Identified* (1920), J. Thomas Looney became the first published "Oxfordian" when he proposed Edward de Vere, seventeenth earl of Oxford, as the secret author of Shakespeare's plays. Also for Oxford and his "authorship" there are today dedicated societies, articles, journals, and books. Less popular candidates – Queen Elizabeth and Christopher Marlowe among them – have had adherents, but the movement seems to have divided into two main contending factions, Baconian and Oxfordian. (For further details on all the candidates for "Shakespeare," see S. Schoenbaum, *Shakespeare's Lives,* 2nd ed., 1991.)

The Baconians, the Oxfordians, and supporters of other candidates have one trait in common – they are snobs. Every pro-Bacon or pro-Oxford tract sooner or later claims that the historical William Shakespeare of Stratford-upon-Avon could not have written the plays because he could not have had the training, the university education, the experience, and indeed the imagination or background their author supposedly possessed. Only a learned genius like Bacon or an aristocrat like Oxford could have written such fine plays. (As it happens, lucky male children of the middle class had access to better education than most aristocrats in Elizabethan England – and Oxford was not particularly well educated.) Shakespeare received in the Stratford grammar school a formal education that would daunt many college graduates today; and popular rival playwrights such as the very learned Ben Jonson and George Chapman, both of whom also lacked university training, achieved great artistic success, without being taken as Bacon or Oxford.

Besides snobbery, one other quality characterizes the authorship controversy: lack of evidence. A great deal of testimony from Shakespeare's time shows that Shakespeare wrote Shakespeare's plays and that his contemporaries recognized them as distinctive and distinctly superior. (Some of that contemporary evidence is collected in E. K. Chambers, *William Shakespeare: A Study of Facts and Problems,* 2 vols., 1930.) Since that testimony comes from Shakespeare's enemies and theatrical competitors as well as from his co-workers and from the Elizabethan equivalent of literary journalists, it seems unlikely that, if any of these sources had known he was a fraud, they would have failed to record that fact.

Books About Shakespeare's Theater

Useful scholarly studies of theatrical life in Shakespeare's day include: G. E. Bentley, *The Jacobean and Caroline Stage,* 7 vols. (1941-68), and the same author's *The Professions of Dramatist and Player in Shakespeare's Time, 1590-1642* (1986); E. K. Chambers, *The Elizabethan Stage,* 4 vols. (1923); R. A. Foakes, *Illustrations of the English Stage, 1580-1642* (1985); Andrew Gurr, *The Shakespearean Stage,* 3rd ed. (1992), and the same author's *Play-going in Shakespeare's London,* 2nd ed. (1996); Edwin Nungezer, *A Dictionary of Actors* (1929); Carol Chillington Rutter, ed., *Documents of the Rose Playhouse* (1984).

Books About Shakespeare's Life

The following books provide scholarly, documented accounts of Shakespeare's life: G. E. Bentley, *Shakespeare: A Biographical Handbook* (1961); E. K. Chambers, *William Shakespeare: A Study of Facts and Problems,* 2 vols. (1930); S. Schoenbaum, *William Shakespeare: A Compact Documentary Life* (1977); and *Shakespeare's Lives,* 2nd ed. (1991), by the same author. Many scholarly editions of Shakespeare's complete works print brief compilations of essential dates and events. References to Shakespeare's works up to 1700 are collected in C. M. Ingleby et al., *The Shakespeare Allusion-Book,* rev. ed., 2 vols. (1932).

The Texts of Shakespeare

AS FAR AS WE KNOW, only one manuscript conceivably in Shakespeare's own hand may (and even this is much disputed) exist: a few pages of a play called *Sir Thomas More,* which apparently was never performed. What we do have, as later readers, performers, scholars, students, are printed texts. The earliest of these survive in two forms: quartos and folios. Quartos (from the Latin for "four") are small books, printed on sheets of paper that were then folded twice, to make four leaves or eight pages. When these were bound together, the result was a squarish, eminently portable volume that sold for the relatively small sum of sixpence (translating in modern terms to about $5.00). In folios, on the other hand, the sheets are folded only once, in half, producing large, impressive volumes taller than they are wide. This was the format for important works of philosophy, science, theology, and literature (the major precedent for a folio Shakespeare was Ben Jonson's *Works,* 1616). The decision to print the works of a popular playwright in folio is an indication of how far up on the social scale the theatrical profession had come during Shakespeare's lifetime. The Shakespeare folio was an expensive book, selling for between fifteen and eighteen shillings, depending on the binding (in modern terms, from about $150 to $180). Twenty Shakespeare plays of the thirty-seven that survive first appeared in quarto, seventeen of which appeared during Shakespeare's lifetime; the rest of the plays are found only in folio.

The First Folio was published in 1623, seven years after Shakespeare's death, and was authorized by his fellow actors, the co-owners of the King's Men. This publication was certainly a mark of the company's enormous respect for Shakespeare; but it was also a way of turning the old plays, most of which were no longer current in the play-house, into ready money (the folio includes only Shakespeare's plays, not his sonnets or other nondramatic verse). Whatever the motives behind the publication of the folio, the texts it preserves constitute the basis for almost all later editions of the playwright's works. The texts, however, differ from those of the earlier quartos, sometimes in minor respects but often significantly – most strikingly in the two texts of *King Lear,* but also in important ways in *Hamlet, Othello,* and *Troilus and Cressida.* (The variants are recorded in the textual notes to each play in the new Pelican series.) The differences in these texts represent, in a sense, the essence of theater: the texts of plays were initially not intended for publication. They were scripts, designed for the actors to perform – the principal life of the play at this period was in performance. And it follows that in Shakespeare's theater the playwright typically had no say either in how his play was performed or in the disposition of his text – he was an employee of the company. The authoritative figures in the theatrical enterprise were the shareholders in the company, who were for the most part the major actors. They decided what plays were to be done; they hired the playwright and often gave him an outline of the play they wanted him to write. Often, too, the play was a collaboration: the company would retain a group of writers, and parcel out the scenes among them. The resulting script was then the property of the company, and the actors would revise it as they saw fit during the course of putting it on stage. The resulting text belonged to the company. The playwright had no rights in it once he had been paid. (This system survives largely intact in the movie industry, and most of the playwrights of Shakespeare's time were as anonymous as most screenwriters are today.) The script could also, of course, continue to change as the tastes of audiences and the requirements of the actors changed. Many – perhaps most – plays were revised when they were reintroduced after any substantial absence from the repertory, or when they were performed by a company different from the one that originally commissioned the play.

Shakespeare was an exceptional figure in this world because he was not only a shareholder and actor in his company, but also its leading playwright – he was literally his own boss. He had, moreover, little interest in the publication of his plays, and even those that appeared during his lifetime with the authorization of the company show no signs of any editorial concern on the part of the author. Theater was, for Shakespeare, a fluid and supremely responsive medium – the very opposite of the great classic canonical text that has embodied his works since 1623.

The very fluidity of the original texts, however, has meant that Shakespeare has always had to be edited. Here is an example of how problematic the editorial project inevitably is, a passage from the most famous speech in *Romeo and Juliet,* Juliet's balcony soliloquy beginning "O Romeo, Romeo, wherefore art thou Romeo?" Since the eighteenth century, the standard modern text has read,

> What's Montague? It is nor hand, nor foot,
> Nor arm, nor face, nor any other part
> Belonging to a man. O be some other name!
> What's in a name? That which we call a rose
> By any other name would smell as sweet.
> (II.2.40-44)

Editors have three early texts of this play to work from, two quarto texts and the folio. Here is how the First Quarto (1597) reads:

> Whats *Mountague?* It is nor hand nor foote,
> Nor arme, nor face, nor any other part.
> Whats in a name? That which we call a Rose,
> By any other name would smell as sweet:

Here is the Second Quarto (1599):

> Whats *Mountague?* it is nor hand nor foote,
> Nor arme nor face, ô be some other name
> Belonging to a man.
> Whats in a name that which we call a rose,
> By any other word would smell as sweete,

And here is the First Folio (1623):

> What's *Mountague?* it is nor hand nor foote,
> Nor arme, nor face, O be some other name
> Belonging to a man.
> What? in a names that which we call a Rose,
> By any other word would smell as sweete,

There is in fact no early text that reads as our modern text does – and this is the most famous speech in the play. Instead, we have three quite different texts, all of which are clearly some version of the same speech, but none of which seems to us a final or satisfactory version. The transcendently beautiful passage in modern editions is an editorial invention: editors have succeeded in conflating and revising the three versions into something we recognize as great poetry. Is this what Shakespeare "really" wrote? Who can say? What we can say is that Shakespeare always had performance, not a book, in mind.

Books About the Shakespeare Texts

The standard study of the printing history of the First Folio is W. W. Greg, *The Shakespeare First Folio* (1955). J. K. Walton, *The Quarto Copy for the First Folio of Shakespeare* (1971), is a useful survey of the relation of the quartos to the folio. The second edition of Charlton Hinman's *Norton Facsimile* of the First Folio (1996), with a new introduction by Peter Blayney, is indispensable. Stanley Wells, Gary Taylor, John Jowett, and William Montgomery, *William Shakespeare: A Textual Companion*, keyed to the Oxford text, gives a comprehensive survey of the editorial situation for all the plays and poems.

THE GENERAL EDITORS

Introduction

*R*ICHARD *II*, PERFORMED as early as 1595, and first printed in 1597, covers the period between April 1398, when Richard (1367-1400) arrived at Windsor and set a date for the trial by combat between Bolingbroke and Mowbray, and February or March 1400, when Richard's body was displayed in London. Like Shakespeare's other "history plays," which might include the plays set in Rome as well as England, this one tells a familiar story drawn from more or less accurate historical accounts. Shakespeare took his basic events and characters from the second edition of Raphael Holinshed's *The Chronicles of England, Scotland, and Ireland* (1586–87). He may also have drawn on other versions of Richard's story: in Edward Hall's *The Union of the Two Noble and Illustrate Families of Lancaster and York* (1548); Sir Jean Froissart's *The Cronycles of Englande* (translated into English in 1523-25); some French accounts that treated Richard more sympathetically; *A Mirror for Magistrates* (1554?-87), an eclectic compilation of stories of the rise and fall of rulers; Samuel Daniel's *The First Four Books of the Civil Wars Between the Two Houses of Lancaster and York* (1595); and *Woodstock* (c. 1592-93), a play depicting the murder of the Duke of Gloucester.

In comedies, the past throws up obstacles that lovers must overcome in order to achieve maturity and marriage; in tragedies, the past, as manifested in a ghostly father or a past error, haunts the protagonists and limits their options. The "past is prologue" to history plays, giving them their purpose – to dramatize what once happened – and their shape. A history play is all backstory, about a past that is understood as having some relevance to the present. Since *Richard II* is usually read as the foundation of a sequence of history plays that goes on to include *Henry IV,* parts 1 and 2, and *Henry V,* the play, in terms of Shakespeare's vision and career, gestures not backward but forward. History and the plays now known as "the Henriad" follow a trajectory that heads toward the dynasty Bolingbroke founds by supplanting Richard. Given this Henrician momentum, Richard's defeat is the necessary pre-text, and Richard seems obsolete and doomed. To wish Richard had kept his throne is to resist history's progression and the plays' focus.

If *Richard II* is backstory for the Tudor regime, it also quite self-consciously and even confusingly alludes to its own backstory: grievances that are articulated as powerful but not made wholly clear. In the play's bewildering first scene, Richard presides over a confrontation between Thomas Mowbray, Duke of Norfolk, and Henry Bolingbroke, Duke of Hereford, who is the king's cousin. For all of the quaint "rites of knighthood," the men's anger at each other is clear (I.1.75). But it will take most readers or spectators a scene or two, and probably some careful consultation of notes in their edition or program, to understand exactly what is at issue. In that process, they will also gradually come to understand that Richard is not just a judge here; he is deeply implicated in the source of conflict between these two nobles. Bolingbroke accuses Mowbray of a whole catalogue of offenses: appropriating for his own use money intended to pay troops, every treason plotted for the last eighteen years, and the murder of Thomas, Duke of Gloucester, Richard's uncle. This last charge is the one with the longest reach. John of Gaunt, Bolingbroke's father, admits to some complicity in the murder, at least in his failure to avenge it; Bolingbroke later accuses Aumerle of involvement. The person at the heart of these accusations, however, is Richard, since Mowbray presumably acted on Richard's order. Bolingbroke claims that Mowbray "Sluiced out" Gloucester's "innocent soul through streams of blood" (103); Gloucester's wife claims that he was cut off by "murder's bloody

ax" (I.2.21). If Richard ordered Mowbray to kill Gloucester, then that murder cannot be viewed as treason against
Richard. Yet Richard's guilt on this charge is never really
made clear. Gaunt accuses Richard of consuming his family's blood: "That blood already, like the pelican, / Hast
thou tapped out and drunkenly caroused" (II.1.126-27).
Gaunt turns the conventional image of selfless nurture, a
parent who feeds its brood from a wound in its breast, to
one of dissolute cannibalism by shifting the focus onto
the child who feeds at its parent's expense. Despite the
fact that, in the first few scenes, Richard seems admirably
reasonable – rising above the rage of the combatants, urging them to make peace rather than fight, imposing banishment as a way to avoid "civil wounds plowed up with
neighbors' sword" (I.3.128) – all of his accusers depict
Richard as a king whose hands are bloodstained. But they
do not spell out responsibility in the clear way that they
would need to in a criminal trial. Instead, a vague sense of
Richard's guilt creeps in at the same time that we begin to
see enacted before us Richard's greed.

Richard, we rapidly discover, is a flawed king. He is ex-
travagant and wasteful; having emptied the treasury, he
has no scruples about how he acquires more funds – bur-
dening his subjects, mortgaging the future, and, in
Northumberland's words, pawning the crown to finance
"too great a court / And liberal largess" (I.4.43-44) and a
"rash fierce blaze of riot" (II.1.33). He is callous in the
face of grief, age, eloquence, and death, turning from the
news of Gaunt's death to say, "So much for that. Now for
our Irish wars" (155). Ignoring the advice of his elders, he
relies on favorites who have little claim to their positions
as his confidants and counselors. He robs nobles to give
lavish gifts to his friends. Bolingbroke later charges these
favorites with exerting a sexual power over Richard, dis-
tracting him from the business of begetting an heir:

You have in manner with your sinful hours
Made a divorce betwixt his queen and him,

> Broke the possession of a royal bed,
> And stained the beauty of a fair queen's cheeks
> With tears drawn from her eyes by your foul wrongs.
>
> (III.1.11-15)

Attacking a sovereign's "evil counselors" was a common way of indirectly attacking a sovereign himself or herself. Such attacks express anxiety about the disturbing redistributions of power that may attend the bodily intimacy between sovereign and favorite. In the play, this charge serves as one more way of articulating how Richard misdirects his energies and mistakes his intimates. While Bolingbroke here presents himself as the queen's champion, the resentment that fuels him and the plot stems not from concern over a neglected queen, but from rivalries between men.

In addition to snubbing and exploiting the nobles, Richard disdains the commons. His inability to win the hearts of the commons is a reminder that popular opinion played a role in politics long before elections. Richard has burdened the commons "with grievous taxes / And quite lost their hearts" (II.1.246). He holds Bolingbroke in contempt for his "courtship to the common people": "What reverence he did throw away on slaves, / Wooing poor craftsmen with the craft of smiles" (I.4.24, 27-28). Once he is king, Bolingbroke is, indeed, popular. "You would have thought the very windows spake, / So many greedy looks of young and old / Through casements darted their desiring eyes / Upon his visage" (V.2.12-15). Richard, the consummate actor, must bear the humiliation of being perceived as the lesser performer, who follows "a well-graced actor" on the stage and whose "prattle" is found, in comparison, "tedious." Bolingbroke is also a performer, and, as it turns out, a more appealing one. In this play, kingship is not just a status, an office, or an identity. It is, for Henry as much as for Richard, a role to be played. "King" is not only a noun, but a verb. Richard describes how kings "monarchize" – that is, play the king (III.2.165). He also describes himself as being "kinged" by his imagination and "unkinged" by his remembrance of Bolingbroke (V.5.36, 37).

Thus Richard and Henry emerge as opposites, but also as players in the same game. In some ways they represent different systems of value – Richard the born king who asserts his divine right to reign but who loses the throne to a man who has earned or fought for rather than inherited it; Henry the soldier, patriot, crowd pleaser, and plain speaker. Yet both kings use violence, eloquence, and charm to get what they want. In the end, Bolingbroke simply does so more effectively. Having seized the throne, he proceeds to establish a dynasty; he does not intend to undermine inheritance as a principle of succession but rather to interrupt that process to position himself as the origin of a new line of kings. For him, as for Richard, kingship will be both powerful – "such is the breath of kings" (I.3.215) – and limited. As Henry's own father, John of Gaunt, points out, even a king cannot lengthen the life of an old, sick man. He can only cut short the life of his rivals and opponents; indeed, he must do so if they threaten his hold on the kingship. Is this a play that shows the beginnings of a contractual notion of kingship, by which an irresponsible king relinquishes his right to rule? Or is this a play that ultimately underscores the divine right of kings and questions the use of violence in securing political power? As is so often true of Shakespeare's work, the play is both. It combines frank appraisal of what it takes to command respect, affection, and fear; admiration of Bolingbroke's vigor, purposefulness, and charisma; unease about the alternatives to inheritance in securing successions; and nostalgic mourning for a lost past.

The play is structured around the conflict between two men and the contrasting trajectories of their lives. Shakespeare could have borrowed the classic *de casibus* structure charting the fall of a great man from *A Mirror for Magistrates,* among other sources. But he contrasts Richard's fall with Bolingbroke's rise so that the plot follows two interconnecting lines, one tracing decline and the other triumph. In III.3, Richard announces, "Down, down I come" (178), comments on the fact that Bolingbroke is kneeling, and prompts him to rise to his feet. Richard's image of the twin buckets – his weighted down with cares, tears, and the crown and scepter, Bolingbroke's carried aloft by his ambition – acknowledges that he must sink for Bolingbroke to rise. There can be only one king. Even the speech prefixes in both the First Quarto and the First Folio signal a transfer in sovereignty. This edition more consistently registers a shift in title: the "King" of the first acts is Richard; in Act V, after the deposition, he has become simply "Richard," and Bolingbroke is now identified as "King." Women who married routinely changed their names, as did noblemen who attained a title. For instance, Bolingbroke is sometimes called "Hereford" or the "Duke of Hereford." But the changing titles in this play suggest the profound uncertainty created by political upheaval. Bolingbroke insists on being thought of as Lancaster despite the fact that his banishment and Richard's seizure of his inheritance have disrupted the process by which he would have taken that title. Aumerle has lost his title "for being Richard's friend" and must be called "Rutland" (V.2.42,43). This is a world of such rapid changes in fortune and shifts in allegiance that those on the losing side (such as Richard and Aumerle) are often described as "amazed."

Richard's fortunes alter suddenly. By the end of II.1, we know that Bolingbroke has gathered forces and is poised to land on England's "northern shore" (II.1.288). Returning to England from Ireland, Richard greets the earth "As a long-parted mother with her child" (III.2.8). Richard couples his almost maternal affection for the land with a sorcerer-like invocation of spiders, toads, and adders to poison his enemies, nettles to sting them. In his view, the natural world is at his command and in sympathy with him. He does not need to prune and weed and discipline, as the gardeners suggest, but rather to mobilize a nature sympathetic to his interests. As it turns out, he is as mistaken about his ability to enlist insects and reptiles as he is about his ability to raise troops or win the hearts of the commoners. Hard upon his happy homecoming, Richard learns that the Welsh have gone over to Bolingbroke.

Richard does not, however, simply sink. Richard's final movement is not down but up. His dying words are "Mount, mount, my soul! thy seat is up on high; / Whilst my gross flesh sinks downward, here to die" (V.5.111-12). In these lines, Richard construes his downward movement as enabling a transcendence. Before this final resolution, he rises again, not in terms of worldly fortunes or political power but in that crucial theatrical currency, sympathy. It is as if there are two Richards in the play – the dissolute, greedy, and irresponsible one, about whom we hear complaint, and whom we only briefly witness in action – and the mournful, dignified, long-suffering, uxorious, and eloquent king who emerges in adversity and impotence.

At several points, Richard articulates the theory of the king's two bodies – the mortal body he shares with other humans, and the "pompous," or symbolic, body that transcends his human limitations and allies him with other kings and with God. While Richard's mortal body is subject to defeat and death, his symbolic body is, by this theory, untouchable: "Not all the water in the rough rude sea / Can wash the balm off from an anointed king" (III.2.54-55). As Richard later concedes, however, he has himself surrendered the symbols of his office, thereby betraying the idea of kingship and exposing himself as merely mortal:

> For I have given here my soul's consent
> T' undeck the pompous body of a king;
> Made glory base, a sovereignty a slave,
> Proud majesty a subject, state a peasant.
> (IV.1.249-52)

Richard has colluded with Bolingbroke at every level. First, as York warns him, he sets the dangerous precedent of interrupting "fair sequence and succession" when he seizes Bolingbroke's patrimony and title (II.1.199). At the level of language, Richard participates in the transfer of sun imagery from himself to Bolingbroke. Richard describes himself as the sun (III.2.36-53; III.3.178); Bolingbroke perceives him as the sun (62-67), as does Salisbury (II.4.21). Finally, Richard describes Bolingbroke as the sun who will melt him like a "mockery king of snow" (IV.1.260-62). Even the famous "deposition" scene might be viewed as an abdication, since Bolingbroke does not force Richard from the throne. Instead, he gets him to agree to surrender the crown. York advises Bolingbroke that Richard "with willing soul / Adopts thee heir and his high scepter yields / To the possession of thy royal hand" (108-10). York later reminds Richard that "tired majesty" has led him to "offer" the state and crown to Bolingbroke (178-79). Bolingbroke repeatedly stresses Richard's volition: "I thought you had been willing to resign" (190); "Are you contented to resign the crown?" (200). Northumberland even attempts to persuade Richard to read a list of his "crimes" so that these will prove him to have been "worthily deposed" (227). As Richard himself summarizes, "With mine own tears I wash away my balm, / With mine own hands I give away my crown" (207-8). By acting as if the crown, scepter, and throne are his to renounce, Richard authorizes Bolingbroke's idea of kingship and betrays his own.

Critics have argued that the deposition of a monarch was so disturbing that it had to be suppressed when the play was printed. Perhaps a monarch who willingly surrendered his office, thus suggesting that a claim to the throne was only as good as the vigor, might, and determination of the claimant, was even more threatening. Certainly the murder of a king, which is represented in all of the print versions of the play, is more troubling still. It has long been thought significant that the so-called deposition scene did not appear in print until 1608, when Elizabeth's successor, James I, had been on the throne for five years. But while James was a man with several heirs, he cannot be imagined to have been any more sanguine about treason and regicide than his predecessor. In 1605, he had survived an alleged conspiracy on a grand scale, the Gunpowder Plot. According to most versions of the story, the Catholic conspirators had secreted barrels of gunpowder in the undercrofts of the House of Parliament, planning to blow it up while Parliament was in session, thus killing James I, his wife and male heirs, and virtually all of the most powerful men in the kingdom. In connection to the plot, thirteen were tried and executed, and two were fined and imprisoned. James's mother, Mary Stuart (also known as the "queen of Scots"), had been executed in 1587 after years of imprisonment because she was viewed as an instigator of and inspiration to conspiracy and a threat to Elizabeth's throne. Elizabeth hesitated before the execution and disclaimed it afterward, largely because executing a monarch set so bad a precedent. As Henry says at the end of this play, "They love not poison that do poison need" (V.6.38). James I's son, Charles I, would be beheaded in 1649, on the grounds that he was a tyrant who had betrayed the trust of those he ruled and had thus lost the privileges of a king. James I could not foresee this, of course. However, his profound sense of the threats to kingly power and prerogative led him to defend the divine right of kings in lengthy treatises and through legislation such as the imposition of an oath in which his subjects had to swear their allegiance to him. In 1608, when he had only recently survived the Gunpowder Plot, and when a quarto of *Richard II* first printed the deposition scene, he was probably as sensitive to the dangers of making "sovereignty a slave, / Proud majesty a subject" as Elizabeth had been.

Throughout her long reign, Elizabeth was the target of numerous plots and assassination attempts, in part because there were still hopes, at home and abroad, of returning a Catholic monarch to the throne and restoring Catholicism as the dominant religion in England, in part because Elizabeth's childlessness rendered her successor uncertain. The assumption that the deposition scene was viewed as especially seditious during Elizabeth's lifetime derives from a particular connection between *Richard II* and the Earl of Essex's plot against Elizabeth. In February 1601, Robert Devereux, the second Earl of Essex, who had long been a particular favorite of the queen's but who had fallen out of favor and under suspicion, led his followers into London in an unsuccessful attempt to seize the throne. Several days before, some of Essex's followers had visited members of Shakespeare's company (the Lord Chamberlain's Men) and offered them 40 shillings, a bit more than one day's take at the box office, to perform some version of the story of Richard II – by this time an old play – on Saturday afternoon, the day before the attempted rebellion. Although Augustine Phillips, a shareholder and actor in the Lord Chamberlain's Men, was subsequently called before the Privy Council and questioned, there were no reprisals against the company, nor punishment expressly for those who attended the play. Treason planned and attempted was clearly the more significant offense than treason represented. For his role in the rebellion, Essex lost his head. Evidence suggests that the story of an anointed king's downfall and a usurper's triumph had become associated with Elizabeth and Essex. The crown made considerable efforts to suppress a printed version of Richard II's story, John Hayward's *Life of Henry IV,* first printed in 1599 with a preface addressed to the Earl of Essex.* Thus the subversiveness of this story was not the special province of the drama, nor a particular tribute to the power of Shakespeare's words, but rather an effect of an association that Essex and his followers may have cultivated, not only through performance but through print.

Some of Richard's most eloquent and moving mo-

---

* J. Leeds Barroll, "A New History for Shakespeare and His Time," *Shakespeare Quarterly* 39.4 (1988): 441–64.

ments are those in which he imagines himself as already dead, and then mourns his own loss. In these moments of retrospective nostalgia for himself, Richard positions not only himself, but all kings, as inevitably doomed:

> For God's sake let us sit upon the ground
> And tell sad stories of the death of kings!
> How some have been deposed, some slain in war,
> Some haunted by the ghosts they have deposed,
> Some poisoned by their wives, some sleeping killed –
> All murdered.
>
> (III.2.155-60)

If one takes a long enough view, kings are never survivors. Like everyone else, they inevitably die. But Richard takes a particularly extreme view here, imagining all kings – at least all those worthy of "sad stories" – as "murdered." He begins with deposition, and moves on to defeat in war and then at the hands of one's own victims (he is perhaps wishing at least a few haunted and sleepless nights on Bolingbroke). Richard ends up with a very domestic and passive picture of kings poisoned by their wives and killed in their sleep.

He similarly domesticates his own story when he imagines his wife, Isabel, as a widow, and begs her to transform his experience into an old wife's tale:

> In winter's tedious nights sit by the fire
> With good old folks, and let them tell thee tales
> Of woeful ages long ago betid;
> And ere thou bid good night, to quite their griefs
> Tell thou the lamentable tale of me,
> And send the hearers weeping to their beds.
>
> (V.1.40-45)

In his longing for narrative immortality, Richard resembles tragic heroes, most notably Hamlet, who insist that their stories be told. Yet Richard imagines a sad story, dwelling on his death, not on his heroic life, on the vicis-situdes he endured, not the actions he undertook. Pathetic rather than heroic, his imagined story is also curiously homely – a bedtime story for "good old folks" or those sitting on the ground. Richard is more interested in how he will be represented than in what will actually happen to him. Assuming and anticipating his death, he concentrates on how he will be remembered. Richard thus requests empathy but then distances it from himself. He demands tears not for himself but for "the lamentable tale of me." As Astrophel requests in Sir Philip Sidney's sonnet sequence *Astrophel and Stella,* "Pity the tale of me."

Richard's combination of self-absorption and self-estrangement becomes especially vivid in the scene in which he reads his face in a mirror:

> Was this face the face
> That every day under his household roof
> Did keep ten thousand men? Was this the face
> That like the sun did make beholders wink?
> (IV.1.281-84)

Intentionally or not, this speech echoes the oft-quoted speech from Marlowe's *Dr. Faustus* (first acted in 1594) in praise of Helen of Troy: "Was this the face that launched a thousand ships / and burnt the topless towers of Ilium?" (V.1.1768-69). In both passages, the beholder stands at a remove from the object of contemplation. Faustus's lines juxtapose Helen's beauty to the destruction it caused. Richard's lines contrast the mundanity of his face to the power once invested in it. Could such a face ever have been so powerful? Perhaps not. Richard's fantasy of his own lost popularity and power may be as much a figment as Faustus's vision of the most beautiful woman of all time. Richard repeatedly views his former power as illusory. He instructs Isabel, "Learn, good soul, / To think our former state a happy dream; / From which awaked, the truth of what we are / Shows us but this" (V.1.17-20).

Shakespeare seems to have expanded or invented the women's roles in this play: the conversation between Gaunt and the Duchess of Gloucester (I.2), the maturity of Queen Isabel (other sources suggest she was only eleven when these events took place), and the appearance of the Duchess of York to plead for her son. The marginal position of the female characters is determined by history in several ways: by the fact that the events dramatized here really were about men, and by an idea of history that assumes it to be about the public actions of men and therefore excludes women by definition. This idea of history stands against another possible history. In England, recent battles over succession had focused on women: Henry VIII's disappointment in his wives' difficulty in producing a male heir, and the subsequent divorces and executions; the nine-day reign of Jane Grey, placed on the throne after the death of Henry's one son, Edward VI, in the hope of securing a Protestant succession and preempting the succession of Henry's daughter Mary Tudor; the reign of Mary Tudor, also known as "bloody Mary," who returned the country to Catholicism, but failed to produce an heir and died young (at forty-two); the reign of the unmarried and childless Elizabeth. In the sixteenth century, women were, in fact, central to English politics and to the English succession. Their marginalization in a play like *Richard II* is, then, both a reflection of the history the play purports to dramatize, and, in the choice of this particular story, a suppression of another more recent history, in which the struggle was not between a poetic king and a militaristic one, but between Mary Tudor and Jane Grey, Elizabeth and Mary Tudor, Elizabeth and Mary Stuart.

A widely cited, but possibly apocryphal, story about Elizabeth claims that she objected to the performance of some dramatization of Richard II's history, which "was played 40tie times in open streets and houses," because it drew a disturbing connection between herself and the deposed and executed monarch: "I am Richard II, know ye not that?"* Whether or not this really happened, the story assumes Elizabeth's ability to identify with a male character and, by doing so, to reinsert herself into a historical narrative that had been designed to shunt women to the margins, to remember the past as a struggle between men – even, in the case of the Essex rebellion, to literally replace Elizabeth with a man.

In *Richard II,* all the women are, unsurprisingly, wives and mothers. As such, they might be seen as crucial to the vital political project of providing for succession. Yet, in the world of the play, mothers seem irrelevant to that project. In the Duchess of Gloucester's famous speech about the "seven vials of [Edward III's] sacred blood" (I.2.12), she presents children as containers for the blood their fathers pass down to them. No mother figures here. While Bolingbroke's usurpation of the throne temporarily bypasses reproduction as the only means of succession, he will found a dynasty and pass this throne on to his own son, a son whose mother is never mentioned. Thus the play does not associate maternity with political power, although the two might be viewed as connected. The women here breed only sorrow. Queen Isabel's fevered imagination ("conceit") conceives and bears a monster in Bolingbroke's treasonous plot. Just after she confides her "heavy" sadness and "unborn sorrow" to Bushy, she learns that Bolingbroke has returned to the country bearing arms and is rapidly acquiring allies. As a consequence, Green, who has brought her the news, is "the midwife to my woe," Bolingbroke the heir born to her sorrow, and she "a gasping new-delivered mother" (II.2.62, 65). To be a queen in this play is to be sad, beweeping both true and imaginary griefs. As Isabel proclaims, "I cannot but be sad" (30). All of the women in the play are grieving: the Duchess of Gloucester over her murdered husband; Isabel over her forsaken bed, her fears, and then her knowledge

* William Lambarde, John Nichols, *The Progresses and Public Processions of Queen Elizabeth,* 3 vols. (London: John Nichols and Son, 1823; originally pub. 1783), 3: 552.

of Richard's downfall. Powerless to redress their grievances, the women can only urge men to seek revenge.

The Duchess of York also has cause for grief: her husband levels a charge of treason against her son; her son is,
indeed, implicated in a plot to restore Richard. She differs
from the other women in the play, however, because she
does not just stand on the sidelines wringing her hands.
She gets on a horse and races to Windsor Castle, where
her husband and son are both making their cases before
Henry. In taking action, intervening rather than just complaining, the duchess threatens to destabilize the play's
tone. When she, a "shrill-voiced suppliant" and "A woman,
and thy aunt, great king," bangs at the door demanding
entrance and a chance to defend her son, King Henry
comments, "Our scene is altered from a serious thing"
(V.3.75,76,79). Something about her entrance leavens the
proceedings. Her emphasis on her body and her feelings is
undignified, disorderly – and effective. She speaks "from
her breast" and on her knees; her husband refers to her
"old dugs"; she imagines herself a wet nurse to the infant
Henry. She endeavors to "alter the scene" from a tragic
one, in which a father turns in his son, who is then executed for treason, to a comic one, in which a mother
humbles herself to save her son's life. She succeeds.

Thus, if Richard's deposition allies him to women, that
association is a complicated one. As soon as Bolingbroke
challenges him, Richard rapidly retreats to a position he
shares with most of the play's female characters – that is,
he laments but does not act to change his fate. Isabel's
only chance to reverse the course of events, and to maintain her status as queen, lies in Richard's action; as a consequence, she chastises him, "wilt thou pupil-like / Take
the correction mildly, kiss the rod"? (V.1.31-32). But this
is a play in which children rebel against their parents, and
the Duchess of York, at least, displays the capacity for
bold action. So to view Richard like a child or like a
woman does not explain that much about him. Further-
more, if Richard endures a fate he does not think he can

alter, that is a position he shares with Jesus Christ as well as with Isabel or the Duchess of Gloucester. Finally, Richard reclaims his compromised manhood through violence. Having valued himself for his own suffering, Richard ends his life in the kind of violent action in which we have never before seen him engaged. He murders two of his assassins. In the end, what is most interesting about Richard is his ability to take a range of actions, some typically associated with men (such as killing his assassins), some typically associated with women (such as assessing himself in the mirror or engaging in a "woman's war" of words, I.1.48), some described as feminine (such as suffering and lamenting the vicissitudes of fortune), but in fact practiced by everyone. He loves his male friends, Bushy, Bagot, and Green, and, in adversity, loves his wife as well. He is imperious and pathetic, boastful and self-pitying, regal and humble, passive and active, all at once.

Gender matters in this play not only in terms of the contests between men, the absent presence of Elizabeth I, marginalized maternity, or the mobility of Richard's gender positions. Gender pervades the play even more subtly, providing a language for the disorder of civil war. Scroop, for instance, describes the chaos Bolingbroke's rebellion has created in terms of generational and gender inversion:

Whitebeards have armed their thin and hairless scalps
Against thy majesty. Boys with women's voices
Strive to speak big, and clap their female joints
In stiff unwieldy arms against thy crown.
* * * * * * * *
Yea, distaff women manage rusty bills
Against thy seat. Both young and old rebel,
And all goes worse than I have power to tell.
(III.2.112-20)

Carlisle predicts that a consequence of Richard's deposition will be "kin with kin and kind with kind" at odds, "Disorder, horror, fear, and mutiny" (IV.1.141, 142). "That

England that was wont to conquer others / Hath made a shameful conquest of itself" (II.1.65-66). In the rift between Aumerle and York, this is just what we see (V.2). If the Duchess of York's intervention is tantamount to "distaff women [managing] rusty bills," it is also an inversion that limits the damage caused by the generational, interfamilial conflict that is civil war.

It might be argued that the central character of the histories is not a human, such as Richard or Henry, but England, an England gendered feminine, as has been much remarked. Bolingbroke calls England's ground "My mother, and my nurse" (I.3.307). Gaunt's famous description of the island calls it a "nurse" and a "teeming womb of royal kings" (II.1.51). Describing the country as a woman, a commonplace in the period, works here to explain the affection men have for their homeland, their sorrow at the prospect of eating "the bitter bread of banishment" (III.1.21), their desire for it, their loyalty to it, their need to protect it from the incursions of other men. For if England is a mother, it is also a virgin whose identity even at the level of geography is defined by impregnability. In his famous paean to England, Gaunt dwells on the impermeability of the island's natural boundaries: "This fortress built by nature for herself / Against infection and the hand of war" (II.1.43-44). England's pristine beauty is not only nature's work, however; it must be husbanded. One of the gardener's men, for instance, laments, "our sea-wallèd garden, the whole land, / Is full of weeds, her fairest flowers choked up, / Her fruit trees all unpruned, her hedges ruined, / Her knots disordered, and her wholesome herbs / Swarming with caterpillars" (III.4.43-47). Those who praise England most warmly also view it as on the brink of destruction. Yet Richard, the bad son and the lazy husband, for all his neglect of this once fertile and discrete land, also has a reverent affection for "our England" (I.4.35), "my earth" (III.2.10). His expression of this feeling (in III.2), through caressing and saluting the earth on his return from Ireland, marks both the beginning of his slide from power – his lowness as he crouches down to pat the earth – and the beginning of his rise in our estimation, since it turns out that he does care about "this England." In the coming centuries, the idea that people love the country of their birth, and that such love is simultaneously deeply personal and greater than self-interest or family feeling, would become a powerful fiction: fueling the rise of nationalism and justifying imperialism and colonialism, genocide and rebellion. At moments, *Richard II* antici-pates these developments, suggesting that, in the end, in-dividual rulers do not really matter. Kings die, even those as vigorous as Bolingbroke, and become sad tales or fa-mous histories. What matters is the country they serve. For if England can be imagined as a character in Shake-speare's histories, then she is the one of all this large cast who endures, for good or ill.

FRANCES E. DOLAN
Miami University, Ohio

Note on the Text

THIS EDITION IS BASED on the First Quarto – or small, single-play edition – of *Richard II*. The First Quarto was entered into the Stationers' Register on August 29, 1597. It is sometimes claimed that this quarto was printed from an author's manuscript. Additional quartos were printed in 1598 (twice), 1608, and 1615. Like most other editors, I add some 160 lines (IV.1.154-318) from the folio of 1623, the first compilation of Shakespeare's works, published after his death. Why were these lines, often called "the deposition scene," not included in the first three quarto printings of the play? Perhaps because censors felt that the deposition – or more accurately, the abdication – of a monarch was too sensitive or inflammatory a topic. Yet these lines might not have been excised from earlier quartos, so much as added to later quartos and the First Folio, perhaps as a result of revision or in response to the performance history of the play. The fact that these lines were not, at first, printed does not necessarily mean that they were not performed whenever the play was. While these lines first appeared in the Fourth Quarto (1608), the folio is widely viewed as the more reliable text; some editors claim that this is because the folio was set from a playhouse copy or promptbook, since it introduces corrections, cuts, and stage directions.

Since the quartos are not divided into acts and scenes, the divisions supplied in this edition follow those in the folio, except that V.3 is split into two scenes, so that the last act has six rather than five scenes (as in the folio). Since the First Quarto provides only minimal stage directions, I have fleshed these out from the folio and elsewhere, indicating any additions in brackets.

Like most editions, this one modernizes and standard-

izes spelling and punctuation, and corrects obvious typo-
graphical errors. I list below any substantive departures
from the copy text – that is, the quarto of 1597 (Q) – and,
for IV.1.154–318, the folio of 1623 (F). The adopted reading in italics is followed in roman by an indication of its
source – usually the quartos of 1598 (Q2 and Q3), of
1608 (Q4), of 1615 (Q5), and of 1634 (Q6), or the folio
and early editors – and then by the reading in the copy
texts, also in roman.

I.1 118 *by my* (F) by (Q)   162–63 *When . . . bids* (Pope) When Harry?
when obedience bids / Obedience bids (Q)   178 *reputation. That* (F)
Reputation that (Q)   192 *parle* (F) parlee (Q)

I.2 23 *mettle* (F) mettall (Q)   47 *sit* (F) set (Q)   58 *it* (Q2) is (Q)

I.3 15 *thee* (Q2) the (Q)   33 *comest* (Q5) comes (Q)   43 *daring-hardy*
(Theobald) daring, hardy, (Q)   133 *Draws* (Q2) Draw (Q)   172 *then
but* (F) but (Q)   180 *you owe* (F) y'owe (Q)   193 *far* (F2) fare (Q)
222 *night* (Q4) nightes (Q)   239 *had it* (Theobald) had't (Q)

I.4 20 *cousin, cousin* (F) Coosens, coosin (Q)   23 *Bagot here, and Green*
(Q6) (not in Q)   52 **s.d.** *Enter Bushy* (F) Enter Bushy with newes (Q)
53 *Bushy . . . news?* (F) (not in Q)

II.1 18 *fond* (Collier) found (Q)   48 *a moat* (Q4) moat (Q)   85 *No, misery* (Q3) No misery (Q)   102 *encagèd* (F) inraged (Q)   113 *now, not*
(Theobald) now not, not (Q)   124 *brother* (Q2) brothers (Q)   130
precedent (Pope) president (Q)   168 *my own* (all but Petworth copy of
Q) *his own* (Petworth copy)   177 *the* (F) a (Q)   257 *king's* (Q3) King
(Q)   277 *Blanc* (Cambridge II) Blan (Q)   280 *The son . . . Arundel*,
(supplied by Malone) (not in Q or F)   284 *Coint* (Halliwell) Coines (Q)
294 *gilt* (F) guilt (Q)

II.2 16 *eye* (F) eyes (Q)   25 *More's* (F) more is (Q)   31 *though on* (Q2)
thought on (Q)   39 *known – what* (Capell) knowen what (Q)   129
that's (F) that is (Q)

II.3 25 *Why,* (Q3) Why (Q)   36 *Hereford, boy?* (Q3) Herefords boy. (Q)

III.2 32 *succor* (Pope) succors (Q)   40 *boldly* (Hudson) bouldy (Q)   72
O'erthrows (F) Overthrowes (Q)   170 *through* (Q2) thorough (Q)

III.3 13 *brief with you to* (F) brief to (Q)   31 *lord* (F) Lords (Q)   33 *parle*
(F) parley (Q)   59 *rain* (F) raigne (Q)   60 *waters; on* (Rowe) water's on
(Q)   119 *a prince and just* (Sisson) princesse just (Q)   202 *hand* (F)
handes (Q)

III.4 11 *joy?* (Rowe) griefe (Q)   26 *pins* (F) pines (Q)   34 *too* (F) two (Q)
55 *seized* (Q3) ceasde (Q)   57 *garden! We at* (Capell) garden at (Q)   80
Cam'st (Q2) Canst (Q)   85 *lord's* (F) Lo: (Q)

IV.1 22 *him* (Q3) them (Q)   43 *Fitzwater* (F) Fitzwaters (Q)   54 *As*
(Johnson) As it (Q)   55 *sun . . . sun* (Capell) sinne . . . sinne (Q)   76 *is
my* (Q3) is (Q)   109 *thee* (Q2) the (Q)   114 *Marry* (F3) Mary (Q)
145 *you* (Q2) yon (Q)   183 *and on* (Q4) on (F)   201 *Ay, no; no, ay;*

(Theobald) I, no no I (F)   255 *Nor* (Q4) No, nor (F)   260 *mockery king* (Q4) Mockerie, King (F)   296 *manners* (Q4) manner (F)   319 *On Wednesday next* (Q4) Let it be so, and loe on Wednesday next (Q)   333 *I will lay* (Pope) Ile lay (Q)

V.1 41 *thee* (Q2) the (Q)

V.2 2 *off* (F) of (Q)   11 *thee* (F) the (Q)   17 *thee! Welcome* (Theobald) the Welcome (Q)   65 *bond* (F) band (Q)   94 *thee* (Q2) the (Q)   116 *And* (Q2) An (Q)

V.3 10 *Whilst* (Capell) Which (Q)   36 *that I may* (Q2) that May (Q)   68 *And* (Q2) An (Q)   75 *voiced* (Q3) voice (Q)   102 *mouth* (Q2) month (Q)   111 KING HENRY (Q2) Yorke (Q)   135–36 *With all my heart / I pardon him* (Pope) I pardon him with all my heart (Q)

V.5 20 *through* (F) thorow (Q)   25 *silly* (F) seely (Q)   27 *sit* (Q3) set (Q)   79 *bestrid* (F) bestride (Q)

V.6 8 *Salisbury, Spencer, Blunt* (F) Oxford, Salisbury, Blunt (Q)   12 s.d. *Fitzwater* (Q6) Fitzwaters (Q)   17 *not* (Q2) nor (Q)   25 *reverend* (Q3) reverent (Q)

The Tragedy of
King Richard the Second

[NAMES OF THE ACTORS

KING RICHARD THE SECOND
JOHN OF GAUNT, *Duke of Lancaster* } *uncles to*
EDMUND OF LANGLEY, *Duke of York* } *the king*
HENRY, *surnamed* BOLINGBROKE, *Duke of Hereford,
    son to John of Gaunt; afterward* KING HENRY
    THE FOURTH
DUKE OF AUMERLE, *son to the Duke of York*
THOMAS MOWBRAY, *Duke of Norfolk*
DUKE OF SURREY
EARL OF SALISBURY
LORD BERKELEY
BUSHY
BAGOT } *servants to King Richard*
GREEN
EARL OF NORTHUMBERLAND
HENRY PERCY, *surnamed Hotspur, his son*
LORD ROSS
LORD WILLOUGHBY
LORD FITZWATER
BISHOP OF CARLISLE
ABBOT OF WESTMINSTER
LORD MARSHAL
SIR STEPHEN SCROOP
SIR PIERCE OF EXTON
CAPTAIN OF A BAND OF WELSHMEN
GARDENER AND HIS MEN
QUEEN TO KING RICHARD
DUCHESS OF YORK
DUCHESS OF GLOUCESTER
LADIES *attending on the queen*
LORDS, HERALDS, OFFICERS, SOLDIERS, KEEPER,
    MESSENGER, GROOM, SERVINGMAN AND OTHER
    ATTENDANTS

SCENE: *England and Wales*]
*

The Tragedy of
King Richard
the Second

❧ **I.1** *Enter King Richard, John of Gaunt, with other*
Nobles and Attendants.

KING

Old John of Gaunt, time-honored Lancaster,   1
Hast thou, according to thy oath and band,   2
Brought hither Henry Hereford, thy bold son,
Here to make good the boist'rous late appeal,   4
Which then our leisure would not let us hear,   5
Against the Duke of Norfolk, Thomas Mowbray?

GAUNT

I have, my liege.

KING

Tell me, moreover, hast thou sounded him   8
If he appeal the duke on ancient malice,   9
Or worthily, as a good subject should,   10
On some known ground of treachery in him?

I.1 A stateroom at Windsor Castle **s.d.** *Gaunt* Ghent (his birthplace) **1**
time-honored venerable; *Lancaster* Duke of Lancaster **2** *band* bond (Gaunt
had promised that his son, Bolingbroke, would appear) **4** *appeal* accusation
(here of treason) made by one who undertook to prove it at the risk of incur-
ring a penalty himself if he did not **5** *our, us* (the royal plural); *leisure* i.e.,
lack of leisure **8** *sounded* questioned **9** *appeal* accuse; *malice* grudge **10**
worthily justly

GAUNT

 As near as I could sift him on that argument,
13 On some apparent danger seen in him
 Aimed at your highness, no inveterate malice.

KING

 Then call them to our presence. *[Exit Attendant.]*
          Face to face,
 And frowning brow to brow, ourselves will hear
 The accuser and the accusèd freely speak.
18 High-stomached are they both and full of ire,
 In rage deaf as the sea, hasty as fire.
  Enter Bolingbroke and Mowbray.

BOLINGBROKE

20 Many years of happy days befall
 My gracious sovereign, my most loving liege!

MOWBRAY

22 Each day still better other's happiness
23 Until the heavens, envying earth's good hap,
24 Add an immortal title to your crown!

KING

 We thank you both. Yet one but flatters us,
26 As well appeareth by the cause you come –
 Namely, to appeal each other of high treason.
28 Cousin of Hereford, what dost thou object
 Against the Duke of Norfolk, Thomas Mowbray?

BOLINGBROKE

30 First – heaven be the record to my speech! –
 In the devotion of a subject's love,
32 Tend'ring the precious safety of my prince
33 And free from other, misbegotten hate,
34 Come I appellant to this princely presence.

---

13 *apparent* obvious 18 *High-stomached* haughty 22 *Each . . . happiness* may each day surpass the happiness of the last 23 *hap* luck 24 *immortal title* i.e., angel or saint 26 *cause you come* matter you come about 28 *what . . . object* what accusation do you make 32 *Tend'ring* being lovingly mindful of 33 *misbegotten* of any other kind than that begotten of love for the king 34 *appellant* as accuser

Now, Thomas Mowbray, do I turn to thee,
And mark my greeting well; for what I speak
My body shall make good upon this earth
Or my divine soul answer it in heaven.
Thou art a traitor and a miscreant,   39
Too good to be so, and too bad to live,   40
Since the more fair and crystal is the sky,
The uglier seem the clouds that in it fly.
Once more, the more to aggravate the note,   43
With a foul traitor's name stuff I thy throat
And wish, so please my sovereign, ere I move,   45
What my tongue speaks my right-drawn sword may   46
  prove.

MOWBRAY

Let not my cold words here accuse my zeal.   47
'Tis not the trial of a woman's war,   48
The bitter clamor of two eager tongues,   49
Can arbitrate this cause betwixt us twain;   50
The blood is hot that must be cooled for this.
Yet can I not of such tame patience boast
As to be hushed and nought at all to say.
First, the fair reverence of your highness curbs me
From giving reins and spurs to my free speech,
Which else would post until it had returned   56
These terms of treason doubled down his throat.   57
Setting aside his high blood's royalty,
And let him be no kinsman to my liege,   59
I do defy him and I spit at him,   60
Call him a slanderous coward and a villain;
Which to maintain, I would allow him odds   62
And meet him, were I tied to run afoot   63

---

39 *miscreant* villain, heretic   43 *note* reproach (of treason)   45 *ere* before
46 *right-drawn* drawn in a just cause   47 *accuse my zeal* cast doubt upon my
ardor or loyalty   48 *woman's war* i.e., war of words   49 *eager* sharp   56 *post*
ride at high speed   57 *terms of treason* (such as *traitor* and *miscreant* in l. 39)
59 *let . . . liege* as if he were not related to the king   62 *allow him odds* give
him the advantage   63 *tied* bound

Even to the frozen ridges of the Alps,
65 Or any other ground inhabitable
Where ever Englishman durst set his foot.
Meantime let this defend my loyalty:
By all my hopes, most falsely doth he lie.

BOLINGBROKE
69 Pale trembling coward, there I throw my gage,
70 Disclaiming here the kindred of the king,
And lay aside my high blood's royalty,
72 Which fear, not reverence, makes thee to except.
73 If guilty dread have left thee so much strength
74 As to take up mine honor's pawn, then stoop.
By that and all the rites of knighthood else,
Will I make good against thee, arm to arm,
77 What I have spoke or thou canst worse devise.

MOWBRAY
78 I take it up; and by that sword I swear
Which gently laid my knighthood on my shoulder,
80 I'll answer thee in any fair degree
Or chivalrous design of knightly trial;
82 And when I mount, alive may I not light
If I be traitor or unjustly fight!

KING
What doth our cousin lay to Mowbray's charge?
85 It must be great that can inherit us
So much as of a thought of ill in him.

BOLINGBROKE
87 Look what I speak, my life shall prove it true –
88 That Mowbray hath received eight thousand nobles

---

65 *inhabitable* uninhabitable   **69** *gage* glove (thrown down in token of defiance; when an opponent picks up the gage he has accepted the challenge)
70 *kindred* kinship   **72** *except* use as an exception   **73** *guilty dread* fear of offending your betters   **74** *mine honor's pawn* i.e., the *gage*   **77** *or . . . devise* or anything worse you can imagine I have said   **78–79** *that sword . . . shoulder* (the king conferred knighthood by laying a sword on the shoulder)   **82** *light* dismount   **85–86** *inherit us . . . as of* make us have   **87** *Look what* whatever   **88** *nobles* gold coins worth 20 groats or about 7 shillings each

In name of lendings for your highness' soldiers,   89
The which he hath detained for lewd employments,   90
Like a false traitor and injurious villain.
Besides I say, and will in battle prove –
Or here, or elsewhere to the furthest verge   93
That ever was surveyed by English eye –
That all the treasons for these eighteen years   95
Complotted and contrivèd in this land   96
Fetch from false Mowbray their first head and spring.   97
Further I say, and further will maintain,   98
Upon his bad life to make all this good,
That he did plot the Duke of Gloucester's death,   100
Suggest his soon-believing adversaries,   101
And consequently, like a traitor coward,   102
Sluiced out his innocent soul through streams of blood;   103
Which blood, like sacrificing Abel's, cries,   104
Even from the tongueless caverns of the earth,
To me for justice and rough chastisement;   106
And, by the glorious worth of my descent,
This arm shall do it, or this life be spent.

KING

How high a pitch his resolution soars!   109
Thomas of Norfolk, what sayst thou to this?   *110*

MOWBRAY

O, let my sovereign turn away his face

---

89 *lendings* pay advanced when regular pay cannot be given   **90** *lewd* base
93 *Or* either; *verge* border, horizon   **95** *eighteen years* (since the commons'
revolt of 1381)   **96** *complotted* conspired, plotted   **97** *head* source **98–99**
maintain . . . good undertake to prove, by ending his wicked life   **100** *Duke
of Gloucester's death* (According to Holinshed, the Duke of Gloucester,
Richard's uncle, conspired against him. As a consequence, Richard had
Gloucester arrested and sent to Calais, where Mowbray was in charge. Under
orders from the king to kill Gloucester, Mowbray first delayed and then
arranged the murder.)   **101** *Suggest . . . adversaries* put his easily persuaded
enemies up to it   **102** *consequently* subsequently and as a result   **103** *Sluiced
out* drained   **104** *like sacrificing Abel's* (Abel, son of Adam and Eve, sacrificed
animals to God; this pleased God more than Abel's brother Cain's offering of
plants. In a jealous rage, Cain killed Abel.)   **106** *rough chastisement* harsh
punishment   **109** *pitch* highest point of a falcon's flight

And bid his ears a little while be deaf,
113   Till I have told this slander of his blood
How God and good men hate so foul a liar!

KING

Mowbray, impartial are our eyes and ears.
Were he my brother, nay, my kingdom's heir,
As he is but my father's brother's son,
118   Now by my scepter's awe I make a vow,
Such neighbor nearness to our sacred blood
120   Should nothing privilege him nor partialize
The unstooping firmness of my upright soul.
He is our subject, Mowbray; so art thou:
Free speech and fearless I to thee allow.

MOWBRAY

Then, Bolingbroke, as low as to thy heart
Through the false passage of thy throat, thou liest!
126   Three parts of that receipt I had for Calais
Disbursed I duly to his highness' soldiers.
The other part reserved I by consent,
129   For that my sovereign liege was in my debt
130   Upon remainder of a dear account
131   Since last I went to France to fetch his queen.
Now swallow down that lie! For Gloucester's death,
133   I slew him not, but, to my own disgrace,
Neglected my sworn duty in that case.
For you, my noble Lord of Lancaster,
The honorable father to my foe,
Once did I lay an ambush for your life –
A trespass that doth vex my grievèd soul;
139   But ere I last received the sacrament,
140   I did confess it and exactly begged

---

113 *slander of* disgrace to   118 *my . . . awe* the reverence due my scepter
120 *partialize* make partial, bias   126 *that receipt I had* the money I received
129 *For that* because   130 *Upon . . . account* for what remains of a heavy
debt   131 *Since last* incurred when   133–34 *I . . . case* (Mowbray perhaps
means that he neglected duty by postponing Gloucester's murder)   139–40
ere . . . it (Catholicism requires that one confess sins to a priest before receiving the Eucharist)   140 *exactly* completely and expressly

Your grace's pardon, and I hope I had it.
This is my fault. As for the rest appealed,   142
It issues from the rancor of a villain,
A recreant and most degenerate traitor;   144
Which in myself I boldly will defend,   145
And interchangeably hurl down my gage   146
Upon this overweening traitor's foot   147
To prove myself a loyal gentleman
Even in the best blood chambered in his bosom.   149
In haste whereof most heartily I pray   150
Your highness to assign our trial day.

KING
Wrath-kindled gentlemen, be ruled by me;
Let's purge this choler without letting blood.   153
This we prescribe, though no physician;
Deep malice makes too deep incision.
Forget, forgive; conclude and be agreed;   156
Our doctors say this is no month to bleed.   157
Good uncle, let this end where it begun;
We'll calm the Duke of Norfolk, you your son.

GAUNT
To be a make-peace shall become my age.   160
Throw down, my son, the Duke of Norfolk's gage.

KING
And, Norfolk, throw down his.

GAUNT   When, Harry, when?
Obedience bids I should not bid again.   163

KING
Norfolk, throw down, we bid. There is no boot.   164

─────────
142 *rest appealed* remainder of the charge 144 *recreant* cowardly 145
Which which assertion 146 *interchangeably* in turn 147 *overweening* conceited 149 *chambered* located 150 *In haste whereof* to speed which proof
153 *choler* anger; *letting blood* (1) bleeding medicinally, (2) bloodshed in
combat 156 *conclude* make terms 157 *no month to bleed* (almanacs prescribed certain seasons as favorable for medicinal bleeding) 160 *shall* will
certainly; *become* suit 163 *Obedience . . . again* the obedience you owe me
dictates that I should not have to beg you 164 *boot* help for it

MOWBRAY
Myself I throw, dread sovereign, at thy foot.
My life thou shalt command, but not my shame.
The one my duty owes; but my fair name,
168   Despite of death that lives upon my grave,
To dark dishonor's use thou shalt not have.
170   I am disgraced, impeached, and baffled here;
Pierced to the soul with slander's venomed spear,
172   The which no balm can cure but his heartblood
173   Which breathed this poison.

KING   Rage must be withstood.
174   Give me his gage. Lions make leopards tame.

MOWBRAY
175   Yea, but not change his spots! Take but my shame,
And I resign my gage. My dear dear lord,
The purest treasure mortal times afford
Is spotless reputation. That away,
179   Men are but gilded loam or painted clay.
180   A jewel in a ten-times-barred-up chest
Is a bold spirit in a loyal breast.
Mine honor is my life, both grow in one;
Take honor from me, and my life is done.
184   Then, dear my liege, mine honor let me try;
In that I live, and for that will I die.

KING
186   Cousin, throw up your gage. Do you begin.

BOLINGBROKE
O, God defend my soul from such deep sin!
188   Shall I seem crestfallen in my father's sight?
189   Or with pale beggar fear impeach my height

---

168 *Despite . . . lives* that will live, in spite of death   170 *impeached* accused; *baffled* publicly disgraced   172–73 *his heartblood/Which* the heartblood of that man who   173 *breathed* uttered; *withstood* resisted   174 *Lions . . . leopards* i.e., kings . . . nobles   175 *change his spots* (refers to the proverbial expression "a leopard cannot change his spots" – that is, people cannot change or be changed)   179 *loam* mud   184 *try* put to the test   186 *throw up* (possibly to the king seated above)   188 *crestfallen* humbled   189 *impeach my height* dishonor my high rank

Before this outdared dastard? Ere my tongue   190
Shall wound my honor with such feeble wrong   191
Or sound so base a parle, my teeth shall tear   192
The slavish motive of recanting fear   193
And spit it bleeding in his high disgrace,   194
Where shame doth harbor, even in Mowbray's face.

[Exit Gaunt.]

KING
We were not born to sue, but to command;
Which since we cannot do to make you friends,
Be ready, as your lives shall answer it,
At Coventry upon Saint Lambert's Day.   199
There shall your swords and lances arbitrate   *200*
The swelling difference of your settled hate.   201
Since we cannot atone you, we shall see   202
Justice design the victor's chivalry.   203
Lord Marshal, command our officers-at-arms
Be ready to direct these home alarms.   205

Exit [with others].

*

∾ **I.2** *Enter John of Gaunt with the Duchess of Gloucester.*

GAUNT
Alas, the part I had in Woodstock's blood   1
Doth more solicit me than your exclaims
To stir against the butchers of his life!

---

190 *outdared* exceeded in daring, faced down; *dastard* coward   **191** *feeble wrong* injury only a weak man would submit to or offer   **192** *parle* parley, truce   **192–95** *my . . . face* I would bite out my offending tongue and spit it in Mowbray's face   **193** *motive* moving part (here his tongue)   **194** *in* to; *his* its (i.e., the tongue's)   **199** *Saint Lambert's Day* (September 17)   **201** *settled* unchangeable   **202** *atone* reconcile   **203** *Justice . . . chivalry* justice point out the true knight by giving him the victory   **205** *home alarms* troubles in England (as distinct from the Irish war)

I.2 John of Gaunt's house   **1** *the part . . . blood* my being his brother; *Woodstock* (the Duke of Gloucester's name was Thomas of Woodstock)

4 But since correction lieth in those hands
Which made the fault that we cannot correct,
Put we our quarrel to the will of heaven,
Who, when they see the hours ripe on earth,
Will rain hot vengeance on offenders' heads.

DUCHESS
Finds brotherhood in thee no sharper spur?
10 Hath love in thy old blood no living fire?
11 Edward's seven sons, whereof thyself art one,
Were as seven vials of his sacred blood,
Or seven fair branches springing from one root.
Some of those seven are dried by nature's course,
Some of those branches by the Destinies cut;
But Thomas, my dear lord, my life, my Gloucester,
One vial full of Edward's sacred blood,
One flourishing branch of his most royal root,
Is cracked, and all the precious liquor spilt,
20 Is hacked down, and his summer leaves all faded,
By envy's hand and murder's bloody ax.
Ah, Gaunt, his blood was thine! That bed, that womb,
23 That mettle, that self mold that fashioned thee,
Made him a man; and though thou livest and
    breathest,
Yet art thou slain in him. Thou dost consent
In some large measure to thy father's death
In that thou seest thy wretched brother die,
28 Who was the model of thy father's life.
Call it not patience, Gaunt; it is despair.
30 In suff'ring thus thy brother to be slaughtered
31 Thou showest the naked pathway to thy life,
Teaching stern murder how to butcher thee.
33 That which in mean men we entitle patience
Is pale cold cowardice in noble breasts.
What shall I say? To safeguard thine own life

---

4 *those hands* i.e., Richard's   11 *Edward* Edward III   23 *mettle* spirit; *self*
selfsame; *mold* material or matter   28 *model* image   30 *suff'ring* permitting
31 *the naked pathway* the path to be open   33 *mean* common

The best way is to venge my Gloucester's death.   36

GAUNT

God's is the quarrel; for God's substitute,   37
His deputy anointed in his sight,
Hath caused his death; the which if wrongfully,
Let heaven revenge; for I may never lift   40
An angry arm against his minister.

DUCHESS

Where then, alas, may I complain myself?

GAUNT

To God, the widow's champion and defense.

DUCHESS

Why then, I will. Farewell, old Gaunt.
Thou goest to Coventry, there to behold
Our cousin Hereford and fell Mowbray fight.   46
O, sit my husband's wrongs on Hereford's spear,
That it may enter butcher Mowbray's breast!
Or, if misfortune miss the first career,   49
Be Mowbray's sins so heavy in his bosom   50
That they may break his foaming courser's back
And throw the rider headlong in the lists,   52
A caitiff recreant to my cousin Hereford!   53
Farewell, old Gaunt. Thy sometimes brother's wife   54
With her companion, grief, must end her life.

GAUNT

Sister, farewell; I must to Coventry.
As much good stay with thee as go with me!

DUCHESS

Yet one word more! Grief boundeth where it falls,   58
Not with the empty hollowness, but weight.
I take my leave before I have begun,   60
For sorrow ends not when it seemeth done.
Commend me to thy brother, Edmund York.

---

36 *venge* avenge 37 *God's substitute* the king by divine right 46 *cousin* kinsman; *fell* fierce 49 *career* charge 52 *lists* arena for trials by combat 53 *caitiff recreant* captive coward 54 *sometimes* late or former 58 *boundeth* rebounds 58–59 *Grief . . . weight* i.e., grief, when let fall, as in conversation, rebounds on the speaker, not because it is hollow but because it is so heavy

Lo, this is all. Nay, yet depart not so!
Though this be all, do not so quickly go.
I shall remember more. Bid him – ah, what? –
66   With all good speed at Plashy visit me.
Alack, and what shall good old York there see
68   But empty lodgings and unfurnished walls,
69   Unpeopled offices, untrodden stones?
70   And what hear there for welcome but my groans?
Therefore commend me – let him not come there
To seek out sorrow that dwells everywhere.
Desolate, desolate will I hence and die!
The last leave of thee takes my weeping eye.   *Exeunt.*

*

∾ **I.3** *Enter Lord Marshal and the Duke Aumerle.*

MARSHAL
My Lord Aumerle, is Harry Hereford armed?
AUMERLE
Yea, at all points, and longs to enter in.
MARSHAL
3   The Duke of Norfolk, sprightfully and bold,
4   Stays but the summons of the appellant's trumpet.
AUMERLE
Why, then the champions are prepared, and stay
6   For nothing but his majesty's approach.
> *The trumpets sound, and the King enters with*
> *his Nobles [Gaunt, Bushy, Bagot, Green, and*
> *others]. When they are set, enter [Mowbray] the*
> *Duke of Norfolk, in arms, defendant [, and*
> *Herald].*

---

66 *Plashy* Gloucester's country seat in Essex **68** *walls* rooms **69** *offices*
workrooms
  I.3 The lists, or enclosed space in which tournaments were held, at
Coventry **s.d.** *Aumerle* (as High Constable of England) **3** *sprightfully and*
bold with spirit and boldly **4** *stays* awaits **6 s.d.** *defendant* (Mowbray is
here the defendant, or the one challenged)

KING
    Marshal, demand of yonder champion
    The cause of his arrival here in arms.
    Ask him his name and orderly proceed
    To swear him in the justice of his cause.   10

MARSHAL
    In God's name and the king's, say who thou art,
    And why thou comest thus knightly clad in arms;
    Against what man thou com'st, and what thy quarrel.
    Speak truly on thy knighthood and thy oath,
    As so defend thee heaven and thy valor!

MOWBRAY
    My name is Thomas Mowbray, Duke of Norfolk,
    Who hither come engagèd by my oath
    (Which God defend a knight should violate!)   18
    Both to defend my loyalty and truth
    To God, my king, and my succeeding issue   20
    Against the Duke of Hereford that appeals me;
    And, by the grace of God and this mine arm,
    To prove him, in defending of myself,
    A traitor to my God, my king, and me;
    And as I truly fight, defend me heaven!   25
      The trumpets sound. Enter [Bolingbroke] Duke of
      Hereford, appellant, in armor [, and Herald].

KING
    Marshal, ask yonder knight in arms
    Both who he is and why he cometh hither
    Thus plated in habiliments of war;   28
    And formally, according to our law,
    Depose him in the justice of his cause.   30

MARSHAL
    What is thy name? and wherefore com'st thou hither,

---

10 *swear . . . cause* (before the trial could begin, the combatant had to swear
that his quarrel was just)   18 *defend* forbid   25 **s.d.** *appellant* (Bolingbroke
is here the appellant, or accuser)   28 *plated* armored; *habiliments* garments
30 *Depose him in* take his sworn statement regarding

Before King Richard in his royal lists?
Against whom comest thou? and what's thy quarrel?
Speak like a true knight, so defend thee heaven!

BOLINGBROKE
Harry of Hereford, Lancaster, and Derby
Am I, who ready here do stand in arms
To prove, by God's grace and my body's valor
38 In lists on Thomas Mowbray, Duke of Norfolk,
That he is a traitor foul and dangerous
40 To God of heaven, King Richard, and to me;
And as I truly fight, defend me heaven!

MARSHAL
On pain of death, no person be so bold
43 Or daring-hardy as to touch the lists,
Except the marshal and such officers
45 Appointed to direct these fair designs.

BOLINGBROKE
Lord Marshal, let me kiss my sovereign's hand
And bow my knee before his majesty;
For Mowbray and myself are like two men
That vow a long and weary pilgrimage.
50 Then let us take a ceremonious leave
And loving farewell of our several friends.

MARSHAL
The appellant in all duty greets your highness
And craves to kiss your hand and take his leave.

KING
We will descend and fold him in our arms.
Cousin of Hereford, as thy cause is right,
So be thy fortune in this royal fight!
Farewell, my blood; which if today thou shed,
Lament we may, but not revenge the dead.

BOLINGBROKE
59 O, let no noble eye profane a tear

---

38 *In lists on* through combat with   **43** *daring-hardy* reckless   **45** *direct . . .*
designs conduct this combat fairly   **59** *profane* abuse (because Bolingbroke's
defeat would mean that he was a traitor)

For me, if I be gored with Mowbray's spear.   *60*
As confident as is the falcon's flight
Against a bird, do I with Mowbray fight.
My loving lord, I take my leave of you;
Of you, my noble cousin, Lord Aumerle;
Not sick, although I have to do with death,
But lusty, young, and cheerly drawing breath.   *66*
Lo, as at English feasts, so I regreet   *67*
The daintiest last, to make the end most sweet.
O thou, the earthly author of my blood,
Whose youthful spirit, in me regenerate,   *70*
Doth with a twofold vigor lift me up
To reach at victory above my head,
Add proof unto mine armor with thy prayers,   *73*
And with thy blessings steel my lance's point,
That it may enter Mowbray's waxen coat   *75*
And furbish new the name of John a Gaunt   *76*
Even in the lusty havior of his son.   *77*

GAUNT
God in thy good cause make thee prosperous!
Be swift like lightning in the execution
And let thy blows, doubly redoublèd,   *80*
Fall like amazing thunder on the casque   *81*
Of thy adverse pernicious enemy.   *82*
Rouse up thy youthful blood; be valiant and live.

BOLINGBROKE
Mine innocence and Saint George to thrive!   *84*

MOWBRAY
However God or fortune cast my lot,
There lives or dies, true to King Richard's throne,
A loyal, just, and upright gentleman.
Never did captive with a freer heart   *88*
Cast off his chains of bondage and embrace

---

66 *cheerly* cheerily   **67** *regreet* greet   **73** *proof* invulnerability   **75** *enter . . . coat* pierce his armor as though it were wax   **76** *a* of   **77** *havior* action   **81** *amazing* stupefying; *casque* helmet   **82** *adverse* opposing   **84** *to thrive* I rely for success on   **88** *freer* more willing

90 His golden uncontrolled enfranchisement,
    More than my dancing soul doth celebrate
    This feast of battle with mine adversary.
    Most mighty liege, and my companion peers,
    Take from my mouth the wish of happy years.
95 As gentle and as jocund as to jest
    Go I to fight. Truth hath a quiet breast.

KING

97 Farewell, my lord. Securely I espy
98 Virtue with valor couchèd in thine eye.
    Order the trial, marshal, and begin.

MARSHAL

100 Harry of Hereford, Lancaster, and Derby,
    Receive thy lance, and God defend the right!

BOLINGBROKE

    Strong as a tower in hope, I cry amen.

MARSHAL   *[To an Officer]*
    Go bear this lance to Thomas, Duke of Norfolk.

[FIRST] HERALD

    Harry of Hereford, Lancaster, and Derby
    Stands here for God, his sovereign, and himself,
    On pain to be found false and recreant,
    To prove the Duke of Norfolk, Thomas Mowbray,
    A traitor to his God, his king, and him,
    And dares him to set forward to the fight.

[SECOND] HERALD

110 Here standeth Thomas Mowbray, Duke of Norfolk,
    On pain to be found false and recreant,
112 Both to defend himself and to approve
    Henry of Hereford, Lancaster, and Derby
    To God, his sovereign, and to him disloyal,
    Courageously and with a free desire
116 Attending but the signal to begin.

MARSHAL

    Sound trumpets, and set forward combatants.

---

95 *gentle* tranquil; *to jest* to mock-fight   **97** *Securely I espy* I am confident that I see   **98** *couchèd* located   **112** *approve* prove   **116** *Attending* awaiting

[A charge sounded.]
Stay! The king hath thrown his warder down.   118
KING
   Let them lay by their helmets and their spears
   And both return back to their chairs again.   120
   Withdraw with us; and let the trumpets sound
   While we return these dukes what we decree.   122
    [A long flourish.]
   Draw near,
   And list what with our council we have done.   124
   For that our kingdom's earth should not be soiled
   With that dear blood which it hath fosterèd;
   And for our eyes do hate the dire aspect
   Of civil wounds plowed up with neighbors' sword;
   And for we think the eagle-wingèd pride
   Of sky-aspiring and ambitious thoughts   130
   With rival-hating envy set on you   131
   To wake our peace, which in our country's cradle
   Draws the sweet infant breath of gentle sleep;
   Which so roused up with boist'rous untuned drums,
   With harsh-resounding trumpets' dreadful bray
   And grating shock of wrathful iron arms,
   Might from our quiet confines fright fair peace   137
   And make us wade even in our kindred's blood:
   Therefore we banish you our territories.   139
   You, cousin Hereford, upon pain of life,   140
   Till twice five summers have enriched our fields
   Shall not regreet our fair dominions   142
   But tread the stranger paths of banishment.   143
BOLINGBROKE
   Your will be done. This must my comfort be –
   That sun that warms you here shall shine on me,
   And those his golden beams to you here lent

---

118 *warder* gilded baton (held by Richard as commander of the trial) **122**
While until; *return* tell, inform; **s.d.** *flourish* trumpet call **124** *list* listen to
131 *set on you* set you on **137** *confines* borders **139** *you our* you from our
142 *regreet* greet again **143** *stranger* alien

Shall point on me and gild my banishment.

KING
148 Norfolk, for thee remains a heavier doom,
    Which I with some unwillingness pronounce:
150 The sly slow hours shall not determinate
151 The dateless limit of thy dear exile.
    The hopeless word of "never to return"
    Breathe I against thee, upon pain of life.

MOWBRAY
    A heavy sentence, my most sovereign liege,
    And all unlooked for from your highness' mouth.
156 A dearer merit, not so deep a maim
    As to be cast forth in the common air,
    Have I deservèd at your highness' hands.
    The language I have learnt these forty years,
160 My native English, now I must forgo;
    And now my tongue's use is to me no more
    Than an unstringèd viol or a harp,
163 Or like a cunning instrument cased up
164 Or, being open, put into his hands
165 That knows no touch to tune the harmony.
    Within my mouth you have enjailed my tongue,
167 Doubly portcullised with my teeth and lips;
    And dull, unfeeling, barren ignorance
    Is made my jailer to attend on me.
170 I am too old to fawn upon a nurse,
    Too far in years to be a pupil now.
    What is thy sentence then but speechless death,
173 Which robs my tongue from breathing native breath?

KING
174 It boots thee not to be compassionate.

---

148 *doom* judgment 150 *determinate* end 151 *dateless* unlimited; *limit* term; *dear* hard, severe 156 *dearer* more welcome; *merit* reward; *maim* crippling injury 163 *cunning* skillfully made 164 *open* out of its case 165 *That . . . harmony* who does not have the skill to play it 167 *portcullised* enclosed by a movable grating 170 *nurse* i.e., a child's earliest caretaker, who might teach the baby its first words 173 *Which* thy sentence, which; *breath* speech 174 *boots* helps; *compassionate* sorrowfully lamenting

After our sentence plaining comes too late.   175
MOWBRAY
   Then thus I turn me from my country's light
   To dwell in solemn shades of endless night.
KING
   Return again and take an oath with thee.
   Lay on our royal sword your banished hands;   179
   Swear by the duty that you owe to God   180
   (Our part therein we banish with yourselves)   181
   To keep the oath that we administer:
   You never shall, so help you truth and God,
   Embrace each other's love in banishment;
   Nor never look upon each other's face;
   Nor never write, regreet, nor reconcile
   This louring tempest of your home-bred hate;   187
   Nor never by advisèd purpose meet   188
   To plot, contrive, or complot any ill
   'Gainst us, our state, our subjects, or our land.   190
BOLINGBROKE
   I swear.
MOWBRAY
   And I, to keep all this.
BOLINGBROKE
   Norfolk, so far as to mine enemy: 193
   By this time, had the king permitted us,
   One of our souls had wandered in the air,   195
   Banished this frail sepulcher of our flesh,   196
   As now our flesh is banished from this land.
   Confess thy treasons ere thou fly the realm.
   Since thou hast far to go, bear not along
   The clogging burden of a guilty soul.   200

---

175 *plaining* complaining   179 *Lay . . . hands* (he addresses both combatants)   181 *therein* in the duty you owe (i.e., they no longer owe duty to the
king once they are banished)   187 *louring* frowning, threatening   188 *advisèd* determined, premeditated   193 *so. . . . enemy* so far as I may speak to
my sworn enemy   195 *One . . . air* i.e., one of us would be dead   196 *sepulcher* tomb

MOWBRAY
  No, Bolingbroke. If ever I were traitor,
  My name be blotted from the book of life
  And I from heaven banished as from hence!
  But what thou art, God, thou, and I do know;
205 And all too soon, I fear, the king shall rue.
  Farewell, my liege. Now no way can I stray.
  Save back to England, all the world's my way.   *Exit.*

KING
208 Uncle, even in the glasses of thine eyes
  I see thy grievèd heart. Thy sad aspect
210 Hath from the number of his banished years
  Plucked four away.
    [To Bolingbroke]
                            Six frozen winters spent,
  Return with welcome home from banishment.

BOLINGBROKE
  How long a time lies in one little word!
214 Four lagging winters and four wanton springs
  End in a word, such is the breath of kings.

GAUNT
  I thank my liege that in regard of me
  He shortens four years of my son's exile.
218 But little vantage shall I reap thereby;
  For ere the six years that he hath to spend
220 Can change their moons and bring their times about,
221 My oil-dried lamp and time-bewasted light
222 Shall be extinct with age and endless night,
223 My inch of taper will be burnt and done,
224 And blindfold death not let me see my son.

KING
  Why, uncle, thou hast many years to live.

---

205 *rue* regret 208 *glasses . . . eyes* your eyes as mirrors 214 *wanton* luxuri-
ant 218 *vantage* advantage 221 *oil-dried* empty; *time-bewasted* spent by
time 222 *extinct* extinguished 223 *taper* candle 224 *blindfold death*
death, like a blindfold

GAUNT
   But not a minute, king, that thou canst give.
   Shorten my days thou canst with sullen sorrow
   And pluck nights from me, but not lend a morrow.
   Thou canst help time to furrow me with age,   229
   But stop no wrinkle in his pilgrimage.   230
   Thy word is current with him for my death,   231
   But dead, thy kingdom cannot buy my breath.

KING
   Thy son is banished upon good advice,
   Whereto thy tongue a party verdict gave.   234
   Why at our justice seem'st thou then to lour?   235

GAUNT
   Things sweet to taste prove in digestion sour.
   You urged me as a judge; but I had rather
   You would have bid me argue like a father.
   O, had it been a stranger, not my child,
   To smooth his fault I should have been more mild.   240
   A partial slander sought I to avoid,   241
   And in the sentence my own life destroyed.
   Alas, I looked when some of you should say   243
   I was too strict to make mine own away;   244
   But you gave leave to my unwilling tongue
   Against my will to do myself this wrong.   246

KING
   Cousin, farewell; and, uncle, bid him so.
   Six years we banish him, and he shall go.
             [Flourish.] Exit [King with his train].

AUMERLE
   Cousin, farewell. What presence must not know,   249

---

229 *furrow. . . . age* i.e., plow furrows or lines into my brow **230** *stop . . .
pilgrimage* prevent no wrinkle that time's course brings **231** *current* valid
234 *party verdict* part of the verdict **235** *lour* scowl **240** *smooth* gloss over
241 *partial slander* accusation of partiality (to my own son) **243** *looked*
waited for a moment **244** *to . . . away* to sacrifice or banish my own son
246 *wrong* injury **249** *What . . . know* what you can't say here

250 From where you do remain let paper show.

MARSHAL
      My lord, no leave take I; for I will ride,
      As far as land will let me, by your side.

GAUNT
      O, to what purpose dost thou hoard thy words
      That thou returnest no greeting to thy friends?

BOLINGBROKE
      I have too few to take my leave of you,
256   When the tongue's office should be prodigal
257   To breathe the abundant dolor of the heart.

GAUNT
      Thy grief is but thy absence for a time.

BOLINGBROKE
      Joy absent, grief is present for that time.

GAUNT
260   What is six winters? They are quickly gone.

BOLINGBROKE
      To men in joy; but grief makes one hour ten.

GAUNT
262   Call it a travail that thou tak'st for pleasure.

BOLINGBROKE
      My heart will sigh when I miscall it so,
      Which finds it an enforcèd pilgrimage.

GAUNT
      The sullen passage of thy weary steps
266   Esteem as foil wherein thou art to set
      The precious jewel of thy home return.

BOLINGBROKE
      Nay, rather every tedious stride I make
269   Will but remember me what a deal of world
270   I wander from the jewels that I love.

---

250 *remain* settle 256 *prodigal* lavish 257 *breathe* express; *dolor* grief
262 *travail* (1) exertion, (2) childbirth, or "labor" (with a pun on "travel," or
journey) 266 *foil* thin, bright metal leaf placed under a gem to heighten its
brilliance 269 *remember* remind; *what . . . world* how far

Must I not serve a long apprenticehood   271
To foreign passages and, in the end,   272
Having my freedom, boast of nothing else
But that I was a journeyman to grief?   274
GAUNT
   All places that the eye of heaven visits
   Are to a wise man ports and happy havens.
   Teach thy necessity to reason thus: 277
   There is no virtue like necessity.
   Think not the king did banish thee,
   But thou the king. Woe doth the heavier sit   *280*
   Where it perceives it is but faintly borne.   281
   Go, say I sent thee forth to purchase honor,
   And not, the king exiled thee; or suppose
   Devouring pestilence hangs in our air
   And thou art flying to a fresher clime.
   Look what thy soul holds dear, imagine it   286
   To lie that way thou goest, not whence thou com'st.
   Suppose the singing birds musicians,
   The grass whereon thou tread'st the presence strewed,   289
   The flowers fair ladies, and thy steps no more   *290*
   Than a delightful measure or a dance;   291
   For gnarling sorrow hath less power to bite   292
   The man that mocks at it and sets it light.   293
BOLINGBROKE
   O, who can hold a fire in his hand
   By thinking on the frosty Caucasus?
   Or cloy the hungry edge of appetite   296
   By bare imagination of a feast?   297

---

271 *apprenticehood* apprenticeship (Apprentices learned a trade by serving under a master. Eventually, having gained *freedom* [l. 273] from the master, they became journeymen [cf. l.274], or beginning craftsmen, who earned their own wages.) **272** *foreign passages* experiences abroad **274** *journeyman* worker for a daily wage, often itinerant **277** *necessity* unchangeable circumstances **281** *faintly* faintheartedly **286** *Look what* whatever **289** *presence* royal audience chamber; *strewed* i.e., the floor covered with rushes **291** *measure* slow, formal dance **292** *gnarling* snarling **293** *sets it light* takes it lightly **296** *cloy* dull **297** *bare* mere

Or wallow naked in December snow
299   By thinking on fantastic summer's heat?
300   O, no! The apprehension of the good
Gives but the greater feeling to the worse.
302   Fell sorrow's tooth doth never rankle more
303   Than when he bites, but lanceth not the sore.

GAUNT
Come, come, my son, I'll bring thee on thy way.
Had I thy youth and cause, I would not stay.

BOLINGBROKE
Then, England's ground, farewell; sweet soil, adieu,
My mother, and my nurse, that bears me yet!
Where'er I wander, boast of this I can,
Though banished, yet a true-born English man.

                                                    Exeunt.

*

❧ **I.4** *Enter the King, with Green, etc. [Bagot], at one
door, and the Lord Aumerle at another.*

KING
We did observe. Cousin Aumerle,
2   How far brought you high Hereford on his way?

AUMERLE
I brought high Hereford, if you call him so,
But to the next high way, and there I left him.

KING
And say, what store of parting tears were shed?

AUMERLE
6   Faith, none for me; except the northeast wind,
Which then blew bitterly against our faces,
8   Awaked the sleeping rheum, and so by chance

---

299 *fantastic* imaginary   300 *apprehension* expectation   302 *rankle* inflict a
painful, festering wound   303 *lanceth not the sore* represses the sorrow and
lets it fester

I.4 King Richard's court   2 *high* proud, haughty   6 *for me* for my part
8 *rheum* moisture, tears

Did grace our hollow parting with a tear.   9
KING
    What said our cousin when you parted with him?   *10*
AUMERLE
    "Farewell!"
    And, for my heart disdainèd that my tongue   12
    Should so profane the word, that taught me craft   13
    To counterfeit oppression of such grief
    That words seemed buried in my sorrow's grave.
    Marry, would the word "farewell" have lengthened 16
    hours
    And added years to his short banishment,
    He should have had a volume of farewells;
    But since it would not, he had none of me.
KING
    He is our cousin, cousin; but 'tis doubt,   20
    When time shall call him home from banishment,
    Whether our kinsman come to see his friends.   22
    Ourself and Bushy, Bagot here, and Green
    Observed his courtship to the common people;
    How he did seem to dive into their hearts
    With humble and familiar courtesy;
    What reverence he did throw away on slaves,
    Wooing poor craftsmen with the craft of smiles
    And patient underbearing of his fortune,   29
    As 'twere to banish their affects with him.   30
    Off goes his bonnet to an oyster wench;   31
    A brace of draymen bid God speed him well   32
    And had the tribute of his supple knee,   33
    With "Thanks, my countrymen, my loving friends";
    As were our England in reversion his,   35

---

9 *hollow* insincere   12 *for* because   13 *that* this experience, described in the preceding clause   16 *Marry* indeed (originally an oath on the name of the Virgin Mary)   20 *'tis* there is   22 *his friends* us of his own rank   29 *underbearing* enduring   30 *affects* affections   31 *bonnet* hat; *oyster wench* woman who sells oysters   32 *brace of draymen* pair of men who drive carts   33 *tribute . . . knee* i.e., he curtsied to them   35 *in reversion* by right of legal succession

And he our subjects' next degree in hope.
GREEN
Well, he is gone, and with him go these thoughts!
38 Now for the rebels which stand out in Ireland,
39 Expedient manage must be made, my liege,
40 Ere further leisure yield them further means
For their advantage and your highness' loss.
KING
We will ourself in person to this war;
43 And, for our coffers, with too great a court
44 And liberal largess, are grown somewhat light,
45 We are enforced to farm our royal realm,
The revenue whereof shall furnish us
For our affairs in hand. If that come short,
48 Our substitutes at home shall have blank charters,
Whereto, when they shall know what men are rich,
50 They shall subscribe them for large sums of gold
51 And send them after to supply our wants,
52 For we will make for Ireland presently.
  Enter Bushy.
Bushy, what news?
BUSHY
Old John of Gaunt is grievous sick, my lord,
55 Suddenly taken, and hath sent posthaste
To entreat your majesty to visit him.
KING
Where lies he?
BUSHY
58 At Ely House.

---

38 *stand out* resist 39 *Expedient* speedy; *manage* plans for controlling 43 *for* because; *too . . . court* too many courtiers (Richard's extravagance was notorious) 44 *largess* gifts 45 *farm* lease (Richard proposes to allow others to collect taxes in exchange for cash in hand) 48 *blank charters* (in effect, loans to the crown on which the amount was left empty, to be filled in by the king's agents) 50 *subscribe them* fill in their *blank charters* (l. 48) 51 *them* the large sums of gold 52 *presently* at once 55 *posthaste* with all possible speed 58 *Ely House* the Bishop of Ely's palace in London

KING

    Now put it, God, in the physician's mind

    To help him to his grave immediately!   *60*

    The lining of his coffers shall make coats   61

    To deck our soldiers for these Irish wars.

    Come, gentlemen, let's all go visit him.

    Pray God we may make haste, and come too late!

[ALL]

    Amen.   *Exeunt.*

*

❧ **II.1** *Enter John of Gaunt, sick, with the Duke of*
    York, etc.

GAUNT

    Will the king come, that I may breathe my last

    In wholesome counsel to his unstaid youth?   2

YORK

    Vex not yourself nor strive not with your breath,

    For all in vain comes counsel to his ear.

GAUNT

    O, but they say the tongues of dying men

    Enforce attention like deep harmony.   6

    Where words are scarce, they are seldom spent in vain,

    For they breathe truth that breathe their words in pain.

    He that no more must say is listened more

        Than they whom youth and ease have taught to   *10*
        glose.

    More are men's ends marked than their lives before.   11

        The setting sun, and music at the close,

    As the last taste of sweets, is sweetest last,   13

    Writ in remembrance more than things long past.

---

61 *coats* coats of mail (with wordplay on *lining*)

    II.1 Ely House   2 *unstaid* uncontrolled   6 *deep harmony* beautiful music
10 *glose* speak empty words in flattery   11 *marked* observed   13 *is sweetest
last* lingers longest in memory

15 Though Richard my life's counsel would not hear,
16 My death's sad tale may yet undeaf his ear.
YORK
    No; it is stopped with other, flattering sounds,
18 As praises, of whose taste the wise are fond,
19 Lascivious meters, to whose venom sound
20 The open ear of youth doth always listen;
    Report of fashions in proud Italy,
22 Whose manners still our tardy apish nation
    Limps after in base imitation.
    Where doth the world thrust forth a vanity
25 (So it be new, there's no respect how vile)
    That is not quickly buzzed into his ears?
    Then all too late comes counsel to be heard
28 Where will doth mutiny with wit's regard.
    Direct not him whose way himself will choose.
30 'Tis breath thou lack'st, and that breath wilt thou lose.
GAUNT
    Methinks I am a prophet new inspired
    And thus, expiring, do foretell of him:
    His rash fierce blaze of riot cannot last,
    For violent fires soon burn out themselves;
    Small show'rs last long, but sudden storms are short;
36 He tires betimes that spurs too fast betimes;
    With eager feeding food doth choke the feeder;
38 Light vanity, insatiate cormorant,
    Consuming means, soon preys upon itself. '
40 This royal throne of kings, this sceptered isle,
    This earth of majesty, this seat of Mars,
    This other Eden, demi-paradise,
    This fortress built by nature for herself

---

15 *life's* lifelong 16 *My . . . tale* my serious dying words 18 *of . . . fond* which even the wise are too fond of 19 *meters* verses; *venom* poisonous 22 *still* always; *tardy apish* aping outmoded foreign fashions 25 *there's no respect* no one considers 28 *will* desire; *with wit's regard* against reason's careful judgment 36 *betimes* (1) quickly, (2) early 38 *cormorant* glutton (from the proverbially hungry seabird)

Against infection and the hand of war,   44
This happy breed of men, this little world,
This precious stone set in the silver sea,
Which serves it in the office of a wall,   47
Or as a moat defensive to a house,
Against the envy of less happier lands;
This blessed plot, this earth, this realm, this England,   50
This nurse, this teeming womb of royal kings,
Feared by their breed and famous by their birth,   52
Renownèd for their deeds as far from home,
For Christian service and true chivalry,
As is the sepulcher in stubborn Jewry   55
Of the world's ransom, blessed Mary's son;   56
This land of such dear souls, this dear dear land,
Dear for her reputation through the world,
Is now leased out (I die pronouncing it)
Like to a tenement or pelting farm.   60
England, bound in with the triumphant sea,
Whose rocky shore beats back the envious siege
Of wat'ry Neptune, is now bound in with shame,
With inky blots and rotten parchment bonds.   64
That England that was wont to conquer others
Hath made a shameful conquest of itself.
Ah, would the scandal vanish with my life,
How happy then were my ensuing death!
YORK
The king is come. Deal mildly with his youth;
For young hot colts, being raged, do rage the more.   70
    Enter King and Queen, etc. [Aumerle, Bushy, Green,
    Bagot, Ross, and Willoughby].
QUEEN
How fares our noble uncle Lancaster?

---

44 *infection* plague and moral contamination   47 *in the office of* as   52 *breed*
ancestral reputation for valor   55 *stubborn* (from a Christian perspective, ob-
stinate in rejecting conversion and resisting the Crusaders)   56 *Mary's son*
Jesus   60 *tenement* land or building leased to a tenant; *pelting* paltry   64
blots i.e., the *blank charters* (I.4.48)   70 *raged* enraged

KING

> What comfort, man? How is't with aged Gaunt?

GAUNT

73   O, how that name befits my composition!
       Old Gaunt indeed, and gaunt in being old.
       Within me grief hath kept a tedious fast;
       And who abstains from meat that is not gaunt?
77   For sleeping England long time have I watched;
       Watching breeds leanness, leanness is all gaunt.
       The pleasure that some fathers feed upon
80   Is my strict fast – I mean my children's looks –
       And therein fasting hast thou made me gaunt.
       Gaunt am I for the grave, gaunt as a grave,
83   Whose hollow womb inherits nought but bones.

KING

> Can sick men play so nicely with their names?

GAUNT

85   No, misery makes sport to mock itself.
       Since thou dost seek to kill my name in me,
       I mock my name, great king, to flatter thee.

KING

88   Should dying men flatter with those that live?

GAUNT

> No, no! men living flatter those that die.

KING

90   Thou, now a-dying, sayest thou flatterest me.

GAUNT

> O, no! thou diest, though I the sicker be.

KING

> I am in health, I breathe, and see thee ill.

GAUNT

93   Now, he that made me knows I see thee ill;

---

73 *composition* body and mind   77 *watched* stayed awake at night   83 *inherits* will get   85 *to mock* of mocking   88 *flatter with* seek to please   93 *see thee ill* (1) see that you are sick, (2) do not see you well because of my own sickness

Ill in myself to see, and in thee seeing ill.   94
Thy deathbed is no lesser than thy land,
Wherein thou liest in reputation sick;
And thou, too careless patient as thou art,
Committ'st thy anointed body to the cure
Of those physicians that first wounded thee.
A thousand flatterers sit within thy crown,   100
Whose compass is no bigger than thy head;
And yet, encagèd in so small a verge,   102
The waste is no whit lesser than thy land.   103
O, had thy grandsire, with a prophet's eye,
Seen how his son's son should destroy his sons,
From forth thy reach he would have laid thy shame,   106
Deposing thee before thou wert possessed,   107
Which art possessed now to depose thyself.
Why, cousin, wert thou regent of the world,
It were a shame to let this land by lease;   110
But, for thy world enjoying but this land,   111
Is it not more than shame to shame it so?
Landlord of England art thou now, not king.   113
Thy state of law is bondslave to the law,   114
And thou –
KING   A lunatic lean-witted fool,
Presuming on an ague's privilege,   116
Darest with thy frozen admonition   117
Make pale our cheek, chasing the royal blood
With fury from his native residence.   119
Now, by my seat's right royal majesty,   120

---

94 *Ill . . . see* I see you poorly because I myself am ill; *in . . . ill* I see evil or sickness in you   102 *verge* compass   102–3 *encagèd . . . land* although the devastation is limited in scope – i.e., confined to Richard's head – it extends as far as his land does   103 *waste* (1) wasteland or desert, (2) tenant's damage to a property   106 *From forth* beyond   107–8 *possessed . . . possessed* put in possession . . . possessed by a devil   111 *for . . . land* since this land alone is your kingdom   113 *Landlord* one who leases out a property   114 *Thy . . . to the law* your legal status is that of subject, not king   116 *ague's privilege* the license a fever affords to rave without consequence   117 *frozen* chilly: (1) cold, (2) caused by a chill   119 *his* its

Wert thou not brother to great Edward's son,
122   This tongue that runs so roundly in thy head
Should run thy head from thy unreverent shoulders.

GAUNT

O, spare me not, my brother Edward's son,
For that I was his father Edward's son!
126   That blood already, like the pelican,
Hast thou tapped out and drunkenly caroused.
My brother Gloucester, plain well-meaning soul –
129   Whom fair befall in heaven 'mongst happy souls! –
130   May be a precedent and witness good
That thou respect'st not spilling Edward's blood.
Join with the present sickness that I have,
133   And thy unkindness be like crooked age,
To crop at once a too-long-withered flower.
Live in thy shame, but die not shame with thee!
These words hereafter thy tormenters be!
Convey me to my bed, then to my grave.
Love they to live that love and honor have.

                    Exit [borne off by Attendants].

KING

139   And let them die that age and sullens have;
140   For both hast thou, and both become the grave.

YORK

I do beseech your majesty impute his words
To wayward sickliness and age in him.
He loves you, on my life, and holds you dear
As Harry Duke of Hereford, were he here.

KING

145   Right, you say true! As Hereford's love, so his;
As theirs, so mine; and all be as it is!

        [Enter Northumberland.]

---

122 *roundly* freely and bluntly   126 *pelican* (believed to feed its young with
its own blood)   129 *fair befall* may good befall   133 *crooked* bent like a
sickle   139 *sullens* bad moods   140 *become* suit   145 *Right . . . his* (the king
purposely takes the opposite of York's meaning)

NORTHUMBERLAND

  My liege, old Gaunt commends him to your majesty.

KING

  What says he?

NORTHUMBERLAND   Nay, nothing; all is said.

  His tongue is now a stringless instrument;

  Words, life, and all, old Lancaster hath spent.   *150*

YORK

  Be York the next that must be bankrupt so!

  Though death be poor, it ends a mortal woe.

KING

  The ripest fruit first falls, and so doth he;

  His time is spent, our pilgrimage must be.   154

  So much for that. Now for our Irish wars.

  We must supplant those rough rug-headed kerns,   156

  Which live like venom where no venom else   157

  But only they have privilege to live.

  And, for these great affairs do ask some charge,   159

  Towards our assistance we do seize to us   160

  The plate, coin, revenues, and movables

  Whereof our uncle Gaunt did stand possessed.

YORK

  How long shall I be patient? Ah, how long

  Shall tender duty make me suffer wrong?

  Not Gloucester's death, nor Hereford's banishment,

  Nor Gaunt's rebukes, nor England's private wrongs,   166

  Nor the prevention of poor Bolingbroke   167

  About his marriage, nor my own disgrace,

  Have ever made me sour my patient cheek

  Or bend one wrinkle on my sovereign's face.   170

---

154 *must be* is yet to be finished   156 *rug-headed* shaggy-haired; *kerns* lightly armed Irish foot soldiers   157 *venom* poisonous snakes; *where . . . else* where no other snakes (i.e., in Ireland)   159 *charge* expense   166 *Gaunt's rebukes* reprimands to Gaunt   167–68 *prevention . . . marriage* (according to Holinshed, Richard forestalled Bolingbroke's marriage to a cousin of the king of France)   170 *bend . . . face* (1) I've never frowned at my sovereign, (2) I've never caused him to frown at me

I am the last of noble Edward's sons,
Of whom thy father, Prince of Wales, was first.
In war was never lion raged more fierce,
In peace was never gentle lamb more mild,
Than was that young and princely gentleman.
His face thou hast, for even so looked he,
177   Accomplished with the number of thy hours;
But when he frowned, it was against the French
And not against his friends. His noble hand
180   Did win what he did spend, and spent not that
Which his triumphant father's hand had won.
His hands were guilty of no kindred blood,
But bloody with the enemies of his kin.
O Richard! York is too far gone with grief,
185   Or else he never would compare between.

KING
Why, uncle, what's the matter?

YORK   O my liege,
Pardon me, if you please; if not, I, pleased
188   Not to be pardoned, am content withal.
189   Seek you to seize and gripe into your hands
190   The royalties and rights of banished Hereford?
Is not Gaunt dead? and doth not Hereford live?
Was not Gaunt just? and is not Harry true?
Did not the one deserve to have an heir?
Is not his heir a well-deserving son?
Take Hereford's rights away, and take from time
196   His charters and his customary rights;
197   Let not tomorrow then ensue today;
Be not thyself – for how art thou a king
But by fair sequence and succession?
200   Now, afore God (God forbid I say true!)
If you do wrongfully seize Hereford's rights,

---

177 *Accomplished . . . hours* at your age   185 *compare between* make such
comparisons   188 *withal* nonetheless   189 *gripe* grasp   190 *royalties* rights
as a member of the royal family   196 *his customary rights* (one of time's
rights was to bring the heir his inheritance)   197 *ensue* follow

Call in the letters patents that he hath   202
By his attorneys general to sue
His livery, and deny his offered homage,   204
You pluck a thousand dangers on your head,
You lose a thousand well-disposèd hearts,
And prick my tender patience to those thoughts
Which honor and allegiance cannot think.

KING
Think what you will, we seize into our hands
His plate, his goods, his money, and his lands.   210

YORK
I'll not be by the while. My liege, farewell.
What will ensue hereof there's none can tell;
But by bad courses may be understood   213
That their events can never fall out good.   *Exit.*   214

KING
Go, Bushy, to the Earl of Wiltshire straight.   215
Bid him repair to us to Ely House
To see this business. Tomorrow next   217
We will for Ireland; and 'tis time, I trow.   218
And we create, in absence of ourself,
Our uncle York Lord Governor of England;   220
For he is just and always loved us well.
Come on, our queen. Tomorrow must we part.
Be merry, for our time of stay is short.   223
             [Flourish.] Exeunt King and Queen [, Aumerle,
                              Bushy, Green, and Bagot].
        Manet Northumberland [with Willoughby and Ross].

NORTHUMBERLAND
Well, lords, the Duke of Lancaster is dead.

ROSS
And living too; for now his son is duke.

202–4 *letters patents . . . livery* royal grants through legal representatives to
sue for possession of his inheritance   204 *homage* avowal of allegiance   213
by with respect to   214 *events* outcomes   215 *Earl of Wiltshire* Richard's
Lord Treasurer; *straight* at once   217 *see* see to; *Tomorrow next* tomorrow
218 *trow* believe   223 s.d. *Manet* remains

WILLOUGHBY
Barely in title, not in revenues.
NORTHUMBERLAND
Richly in both, if justice had her right.
ROSS
228 My heart is great; but it must break with silence,
Ere't be disburdened with a liberal tongue.
NORTHUMBERLAND
230 Nay, speak thy mind; and let him ne'er speak more
That speaks thy words again to do thee harm!
WILLOUGHBY
232 Tends that thou wouldst speak to the Duke of Here-
ford?
If it be so, out with it boldly, man!
Quick is mine ear to hear of good towards him.
ROSS
No good at all that I can do for him;
Unless you call it good to pity him,
237 Bereft and gelded of his patrimony.
NORTHUMBERLAND
Now, afore God, 'tis shame such wrongs are borne
In him a royal prince and many more
240 Of noble blood in this declining land.
The king is not himself, but basely led
By flatterers; and what they will inform,
243 Merely in hate, 'gainst any of us all,
That will the king severely prosecute
'Gainst us, our lives, our children, and our heirs.
ROSS
246 The commons hath he pilled with grievous taxes
And quite lost their hearts; the nobles hath he fined
For ancient quarrels and quite lost their hearts.
WILLOUGHBY
And daily new exactions are devised,

---

228 *great* swollen, heavy 232 *Tends . . . Hereford* does that thou wouldst
speak concern the Duke of Hereford 237 *gelded of* cut off from, castrated of
243 *Merely* purely 246 *pilled* skinned

As blanks, benevolences, and I wot not what;   250
But what, a God's name, doth become of this?   251

NORTHUMBERLAND
Wars hath not wasted it, for warred he hath not,
But basely yielded upon compromise
That which his noble ancestors achieved with blows.
More hath he spent in peace than they in wars.

ROSS
The Earl of Wiltshire hath the realm in farm.   256

WILLOUGHBY
The king's grown bankrupt, like a broken man.

NORTHUMBERLAND
Reproach and dissolution hangeth over him.   258

ROSS
He hath not money for these Irish wars,
His burdenous taxations notwithstanding,   260
But by the robbing of the banished duke.

NORTHUMBERLAND
His noble kinsman. Most degenerate king!
But, lords, we hear this fearful tempest sing,
Yet seek no shelter to avoid the storm.
We see the wind sit sore upon our sails,   265
And yet we strike not, but securely perish.   266

ROSS
We see the very wrack that we must suffer,
And unavoided is the danger now   268
For suffering so the causes of our wrack.   269

NORTHUMBERLAND
Not so. Even through the hollow eyes of death   270
I spy life peering; but I dare not say

---

250 *blanks* blank charters (see I.4.48); *benevolences* "voluntary" loans to the
crown; *wot* know   251 *But . . . this* but what in God's name is he doing with
all this money   256 *hath . . . in farm* has leased the right to collect taxes
258 *dissolution* weakness and decay as a result of overindulgence   265 *sit sore*
press hard   266 *strike* (1) lower sail, (2) strike back; *securely* overconfidently
268 *unavoided* unavoidable   269 *For . . . wrack* since we endured the causes
of the impending disaster and did not intervene

How near the tidings of our comfort is.

WILLOUGHBY

Nay, let us share thy thoughts as thou dost ours.

ROSS

Be confident to speak, Northumberland.
We three are but thyself, and speaking so,
Thy words are but as thoughts. Therefore be bold.

NORTHUMBERLAND

Then thus: I have from Le Port Blanc, a bay
278   In Brittaine, received intelligence
That Harry Duke of Hereford, Rainold Lord Cobham,
280   [The son of Richard, Earl of Arundel,]
281   That late broke from the Duke of Exeter,
282   His brother, Archbishop late of Canterbury,
Sir Thomas Erpingham, Sir John Ramston,
Sir John Norbery, Sir Robert Waterton, and Francis
   Coint,
All these well furnished by the Duke of Brittaine
286   With eight tall ships, three thousand men of war,
287   Are making hither with all due expedience
And shortly mean to touch our northern shore.
289   Perhaps they had ere this, but that they stay
290   The first departing of the king for Ireland.
If then we shall shake off our slavish yoke,
292   Imp out our drooping country's broken wing,
293   Redeem from broking pawn the blemished crown,
294   Wipe off the dust that hides our scepter's gilt,

---

278 *Brittaine* Brittany; *intelligence* information   280 *[The son . . . Arundel,]*
(Many editors add a conjectural line such as this one, on the supposition that
a similar one was cut for political reasons; Elizabeth had imprisoned an Earl
of Arundel in 1585, and had him executed in 1595. In Richard's era, the Earl
of Arundel, not Lord Cobham, *broke from the Duke of Exeter,* l. 281.)   281
broke escaped   282 *late* until recently (he had been deprived of the office by
the pope at Richard's request)   286 *tall* fine; *men of war* fighting men   287
expedience speed   289 *stay* await   290 *The first departing* until after the departure   292 *Imp out* graft new feathers on   293 *broking pawn* the possession of the king's moneylenders   294 *gilt* golden luster (with a pun on
"guilt," the spelling here in Q)

And make high majesty look like itself,
Away with me in post to Ravenspurgh;   296
But if you faint, as fearing to do so,   297
Stay and be secret, and myself will go.

ROSS
To horse, to horse! Urge doubts to them that fear.

WILLOUGHBY
Hold out my horse, and I will first be there.   *Exeunt.*   300

*

∾ **II.2**   *Enter the Queen, Bushy, Bagot.*

BUSHY
Madam, your majesty is too much sad.
You promised, when you parted with the king,
To lay aside life-harming heaviness
And entertain a cheerful disposition.

QUEEN
To please the king, I did; to please myself,
I cannot do it. Yet I know no cause
Why I should welcome such a guest as grief
Save bidding farewell to so sweet a guest
As my sweet Richard. Yet again, methinks,
Some unborn sorrow, ripe in fortune's womb,   10
Is coming towards me, and my inward soul
With nothing trembles. At something it grieves   12
More than with parting from my lord the king.

BUSHY
Each substance of a grief hath twenty shadows,   14
Which shows like grief itself, but is not so;   15
For sorrow's eye, glazèd with blinding tears,
Divides one thing entire to many objects,   17

---

296 *post* haste; *Ravenspurgh* a port on the River Humber (now submerged by
the sea)   **297** *faint* are fainthearted   **300** *Hold . . . and* if my horse holds out
    II.2 Windsor Castle   **12** *With* at   **14** *Each . . . shadows* every true grief
breeds twenty imaginary ones   **15** *shows . . . so* look like grief itself, but are
not   **17** *entire* whole, single

18 Like perspectives, which rightly gazed upon,
    Show nothing but confusion – eyed awry,
20 Distinguish form. So your sweet majesty,
21 Looking awry upon your lord's departure,
    Find shapes of grief more than himself to wail,
    Which, looked on as it is, is nought but shadows
    Of what it is not. Then, thrice-gracious queen,
    More than your lord's departure weep not. More's not
        seen;
    Or if it be, 'tis with false sorrow's eye,
    Which for things true weeps things imaginary.

QUEEN
    It may be so; but yet my inward soul
    Persuades me it is otherwise. Howe'er it be,
30 I cannot but be sad – so heavy sad
31 As, though on thinking on no thought I think,
    Makes me with heavy nothing faint and shrink.

BUSHY
33 'Tis nothing but conceit, my gracious lady.

QUEEN
34 'Tis nothing less. Conceit is still derived
    From some forefather grief. Mine is not so,
    For nothing hath begot my something grief,
37 Or something hath the nothing that I grieve.
38 'Tis in reversion that I do possess;
    But what it is, that is not yet known – what,
40 I cannot name. 'Tis nameless woe, I wot.
        [Enter Green.]

––––––––
18 *perspectives* pictures or designs that (1) emerge into coherence only when looked at from the side (*awry*) or from a particular angle, (2) assume different shapes depending on the angle from which they are viewed   **21** *awry* from the wrong angle   **31–32** *As . . . shrink* even when I try to make myself think about nothing, that nothing itself depresses and frightens me   **33** *conceit* imagination, fantasy   **34** *'Tis nothing less* (1) it is anything but that, (2) imagination is not so easily dismissed   **37** *something . . . grieve* my causeless grief has something in it   **38** *'Tis . . . possess* (1)what I feel is like a property that will devolve upon me later, (2) I can't describe it yet

GREEN

    God save your majesty! and well met, gentlemen.

    I hope the king is not yet shipped for Ireland.

QUEEN

    Why hopest thou so? 'Tis better hope he is;

    For his designs crave haste, his haste good hope.

    Then wherefore dost thou hope he is not shipped?

GREEN

    That he, our hope, might have retired his power   46

    And driven into despair an enemy's hope

    Who strongly hath set footing in this land.   48

    The banished Bolingbroke repeals himself   49

    And with uplifted arms is safe arrived   50

    At Ravenspurgh.

QUEEN   Now God in heaven forbid!

GREEN

    Ah, madam, 'tis too true; and that is worse,   52

    The Lord Northumberland, his son young Henry
      Percy,

    The Lords of Ross, Beaumond, and Willoughby,

    With all their powerful friends, are fled to him.

BUSHY

    Why have you not proclaimed Northumberland

    And all the rest revolted faction traitors?   57

GREEN

    We have; whereupon the Earl of Worcester

    Hath broken his staff, resigned his stewardship,   59

    And all the household servants fled with him   60

    To Bolingbroke.

QUEEN

    So, Green, thou art the midwife to my woe,

    And Bolingbroke my sorrow's dismal heir.   63

---

46 *retired* drawn back   48 *strongly* with strong support   49 *repeals* recalls
50 *uplifted arms* brandished weapons   52 *that* what   57 *revolted . . . traitors*
a rebellious group of traitors   59 *staff* (the sign of his office)   63 *dismal* ill-
omened

64 Now hath my soul brought forth her prodigy;
And I, a gasping new-delivered mother,
Have woe to woe, sorrow to sorrow joined.

BUSHY
Despair not, madam.

QUEEN   Who shall hinder me?
I will despair, and be at enmity
69 With cozening hope. He is a flatterer,
70 A parasite, a keeper-back of death,
71 Who gently would dissolve the bands of life,
72 Which false hope lingers in extremity.
    [Enter York.]

GREEN
Here comes the Duke of York.

QUEEN
74 With signs of war about his aged neck.
75 O, full of careful business are his looks.
76 Uncle, for God's sake, speak comfortable words!

YORK
Should I do so, I should belie my thoughts.
Comfort's in heaven, and we are on the earth,
79 Where nothing lives but crosses, cares, and grief.
80 Your husband, he is gone to save far off,
Whilst others come to make him lose at home.
82 Here am I left to underprop his land,
Who, weak with age, cannot support myself.
84 Now comes the sick hour that his surfeit made;
Now shall he try his friends that flattered him.
    [Enter a Servingman.]

SERVINGMAN
My lord, your son was gone before I came.

YORK
He was? Why, so! Go all which way it will!

---

64 *prodigy* monster   69 *cozening* deceitful   71 *bands* bonds   72 *lingers*
causes to linger   74 *With . . . neck* in armor   75 *careful business* anxious pre-
occupation   76 *comfortable* comforting   79 *crosses* obstacles   80 *to . . . off*
to protect his interests far away   82 *underprop* prop up   84 *surfeit* excess

The nobles they are fled, the commons they are cold
And will, I fear, revolt on Hereford's side.
Sirrah, get thee to Plashy to my sister Gloucester;   90
Bid her send me presently a thousand pound.
Hold, take my ring.

SERVINGMAN
My lord, I had forgot to tell your lordship
Today, as I came by, I callèd there –
But I shall grieve you to report the rest.

YORK
What is't, knave?

SERVINGMAN
An hour before I came the duchess died.

YORK
God for his mercy! what a tide of woes
Comes rushing on this woeful land at once!
I know not what to do. I would to God   100
(So my untruth had not provoked him to it)   101
The king had cut off my head with my brother's.
What, are there no posts dispatched for Ireland?
How shall we do for money for these wars?
Come, sister – cousin I would say – pray pardon me.
Go, fellow, get thee home, provide some carts
And bring away the armor that is there.
                                        [Exit Servingman.]
Gentlemen, will you go muster men?
If I know how or which way to order these affairs,
Thus disorderly thrust into my hands,   110
Never believe me. Both are my kinsmen.
T' one is my sovereign, whom both my oath
And duty bids defend; t' other again
Is my kinsman, whom the king hath wronged,
Whom conscience and my kindred bids to right.
Well, somewhat we must do. Come, cousin, I'll
Dispose of you.   117
Gentlemen, go muster up your men,

―――――
101 *untruth* disloyalty   117 *Dispose of* make arrangements for

And meet me presently at Berkeley.
120   I should to Plashy too,
But time will not permit. All is uneven,
122   And everything is left at six and seven.
     Exeunt Duke [of York], Queen.
     Manent Bushy, [Bagot,] Green.

BUSHY
123   The wind sits fair for news to go for Ireland,
But none returns. For us to levy power
125   Proportionable to the enemy
Is all unpossible.

GREEN
Besides, our nearness to the king in love
128   Is near the hate of those love not the king.

BAGOT
And that's the wavering commons; for their love
130   Lies in their purses, and whoso empties them,
By so much fills their hearts with deadly hate.

BUSHY
132   Wherein the king stands generally condemned.

BAGOT
133   If judgment lie in them, then so do we,
Because we ever have been near the king.

GREEN
Well, I will for refuge straight to Bristol Castle.
The Earl of Wiltshire is already there.

BUSHY
137   Thither will I with you; for little office
138   Will the hateful commons perform for us,
Except like curs to tear us all to pieces.
140   Will you go along with us?

BAGOT
No; I will to Ireland to his majesty.

---

122 *at six and seven* in confusion; s.d. *Manent* remain (plural form) 123–
24 *wind . . . returns* the wind is favorable for sending news to Ireland, but not
for receiving it   125 *Proportionable to* matching that of   128 *those love*
those who love   132 *Wherein* on which grounds   133 *If . . . them* if our
doom depends on them   137 *office* service   138 *hateful* angry

Farewell. If heart's presages be not vain,
We three here part that ne'er shall meet again.
BUSHY
That's as York thrives to beat back Bolingbroke.
GREEN
Alas, poor duke! The task he undertakes
Is numb'ring sands and drinking oceans dry.
Where one on his side fights, thousands will fly.
Farewell at once – for once, for all, and ever.
BUSHY
Well, we may meet again.
BAGOT   I fear me, never.   *[Exeunt.]*
                                    ✳

✢ **II.3** *Enter [Bolingbroke the Duke of] Hereford, [and]*
   Northumberland.

BOLINGBROKE
How far is it, my lord, to Berkeley now?
NORTHUMBERLAND
Believe me, noble lord,
I am a stranger here in Gloucestershire.
These high wild hills and rough uneven ways
Draws out our miles and makes them wearisome;
And yet your fair discourse hath been as sugar,
Making the hard way sweet and delectable.
But I bethink me what a weary way
From Ravenspurgh to Cotshall will be found
In Ross and Willoughby, wanting your company,   10
Which, I protest, hath very much beguiled
The tediousness and process of my travel;   12
But theirs is sweetened with the hope to have
The present benefit which I possess;

II.3 An open place in Gloucestershire   **10** *In* by   **12** *tediousness and process*
tedious process

15 And hope to joy is little less in joy
16 Than hope enjoyed. By this the weary lords
    Shall make their way seem short, as mine hath done
    By sight of what I have, your noble company.
BOLINGBROKE
    Of much less value is my company
20 Than your good words. But who comes here?
        Enter Harry Percy.
NORTHUMBERLAND
    It is my son, young Harry Percy,
22 Sent from my brother Worcester, whencesoever.
    Harry, how fares your uncle?
PERCY
    I had thought, my lord, to have learned his health of
        you.
NORTHUMBERLAND
    Why, is he not with the queen?
PERCY
    No, my good lord; he hath forsook the court,
    Broken his staff of office, and dispersed
    The household of the king.
NORTHUMBERLAND   What was his reason?
    He was not so resolved when last we spake together.
PERCY
30 Because your lordship was proclaimèd traitor.
    But he, my lord, is gone to Ravenspurgh
    To offer service to the Duke of Hereford;
    And sent me over by Berkeley to discover
    What power the Duke of York had levied there;
    Then with directions to repair to Ravenspurgh.
NORTHUMBERLAND
    Have you forgot the Duke of Hereford, boy?
PERCY
    No, my good lord, for that is not forgot

15–16 *hope . . . enjoyed* joy anticipated is almost as good as joy experienced
16 *this* this expectation   22 *whencesoever* wherever he may be

Which ne'er I did remember. To my knowledge,
I never in my life did look on him.

NORTHUMBERLAND
Then learn to know him now. This is the duke.　　　*40*

PERCY
My gracious lord, I tender you my service,　　　*41*
Such as it is, being tender, raw, and young;　　　*42*
Which elder days shall ripen and confirm
To more approvèd service and desert.　　　*44*

BOLINGBROKE
I thank thee, gentle Percy; and be sure
I count myself in nothing else so happy
As in a soul rememb'ring my good friends;
And, as my fortune ripens with thy love,
It shall be still thy true love's recompense.　　　*49*
My heart this covenant makes, my hand thus seals it.　　　*50*

NORTHUMBERLAND
How far is it to Berkeley? and what stir　　　*51*
Keeps good old York there with his men of war?　　　*52*

PERCY
There stands the castle by yon tuft of trees,
Manned with three hundred men, as I have heard;
And in it are the Lords of York, Berkeley, and Seymour,
None else of name and noble estimate.　　　*56*
[Enter Ross and Willoughby.]

NORTHUMBERLAND
Here come the Lords of Ross and Willoughby,
Bloody with spurring, fiery red with haste.

BOLINGBROKE
Welcome, my lords. I wot your love pursues
A banished traitor. All my treasury　　　*60*
Is yet but unfelt thanks, which, more enriched,　　　*61*
Shall be your love and labor's recompense.

41–42 *tender . . . tender* offer . . . immature　**42** *raw* inexperienced　**44** *approvèd* tested and proved　**49** *still* always　**51** *stir* action　**52** *men of war* soldiers　**56** *name* title, reputation　**61** *unfelt* intangible

ROSS
    Your presence makes us rich, most noble lord.
WILLOUGHBY
    And far surmounts our labor to attain it.
BOLINGBROKE
65   Evermore thank's the exchequer of the poor,
    Which, till my infant fortune comes to years,
    Stands for my bounty. But who comes here?
        [Enter Berkeley.]
NORTHUMBERLAND
    It is my Lord of Berkeley, as I guess.
BERKELEY
    My Lord of Hereford, my message is to you.
BOLINGBROKE
70   My lord, my answer is – "to Lancaster,"
    And I am come to seek that name in England;
    And I must find that title in your tongue
73   Before I make reply to aught you say.
BERKELEY
    Mistake me not, my lord. 'Tis not my meaning
75   To rase one title of your honor out.
    To you, my lord, I come (what lord you will)
    From the most gracious regent of this land,
    The Duke of York, to know what pricks you on
79   To take advantage of the absent time
80   And fright our native peace with self-borne arms.
        [Enter York, attended.]
BOLINGBROKE
81   I shall not need transport my words by you;
    Here comes his grace in person. My noble uncle!
        [Kneels.]
YORK
    Show me thy humble heart, and not thy knee,

---

65 *thank's* gratitude is; *exchequer* treasury **70** *"to Lancaster"* i.e., acknowl-
edge me as the Duke of Lancaster, the title I should have inherited from my
father **73** *aught* anything **75** *rase* erase **79** *absent time* time of the king's
absence **80** *self-borne* carried in your own cause rather than the king's **81**
transport send

Whose duty is deceivable and false.   84
BOLINGBROKE
My gracious uncle!
YORK
Tut, tut!
Grace me no grace, nor uncle me no uncle.
I am no traitor's uncle, and that word "grace"
In an ungracious mouth is but profane.
Why have those banished and forbidden legs   90
Dared once to touch a dust of England's ground?   91
But then more why? – why have they dared to march
So many miles upon her peaceful bosom,
Frighting her pale-faced villages with war
And ostentation of despisèd arms?   95
Com'st thou because the anointed king is hence?
Why, foolish boy, the king is left behind,
And in my loyal bosom lies his power.
Were I but now lord of such hot youth
As when brave Gaunt thy father and myself   100
Rescued the Black Prince, that young Mars of men,   101
From forth the ranks of many thousand French,
O, then how quickly should this arm of mine,
Now prisoner to the palsy, chastise thee
And minister correction to thy fault!
BOLINGBROKE
My gracious uncle, let me know my fault;
On what condition stands it and wherein?   107
YORK
Even in condition of the worst degree,
In gross rebellion and detested treason.
Thou art a banished man; and here art come,   110
Before the expiration of thy time,
In braving arms against thy sovereign.   112

---

84 *duty* i.e., act of kneeling; *deceivable* deceitful   **91** *dust* speck   **95** *ostentation* display; *despisèd* despicable   **101** *Black Prince* eldest son of Edward III (he never reigned)   **107** *On . . . it* on what defect in me is it based; *wherein* of what does it consist   **112** *braving* defiant

BOLINGBROKE

As I was banished, I was banished Hereford;
114 But as I come, I come for Lancaster.
And, noble uncle, I beseech your grace
116 Look on my wrongs with an indifferent eye.
You are my father, for methinks in you
I see old Gaunt alive. O, then, my father,
Will you permit that I shall stand condemned
120 A wandering vagabond, my rights and royalties
Plucked from my arms perforce, and given away
122 To upstart unthrifts? Wherefore was I born?
If that my cousin king be king in England,
It must be granted I am Duke of Lancaster.
You have a son, Aumerle, my noble cousin.
126 Had you first died, and he been thus trod down,
He should have found his uncle Gaunt a father
128 To rouse his wrongs and chase them to the bay.
I am denied to sue my livery here,
130 And yet my letters patents give me leave.
131 My father's goods are all distrained and sold;
And these, and all, are all amiss employed.
What would you have me do? I am a subject,
134 And I challenge law. Attorneys are denied me,
And therefore personally I lay my claim
136 To my inheritance of free descent.

NORTHUMBERLAND

The noble duke hath been too much abused.

ROSS

138 It stands your grace upon to do him right.

WILLOUGHBY

139 Base men by his endowments are made great.

YORK

140 My lords of England, let me tell you this:

---

114 *for* as   116 *indifferent* impartial   122 *unthrifts* spendthrifts; *Wherefore* why   126 *first* i.e., before Gaunt   128 *rouse* rout from cover; *chase . . . bay* hunt them to the death   130 *leave* permission   131 *distrained* seized   134 *challenge law* demand my rights   136 *my inheritance of* that which I inherit by   138 *It . . . upon* it's up to you   139 *endowments* inheritance

I have had feeling of my cousin's wrongs,
And labored all I could to do him right;
But in this kind to come, in braving arms,   143
Be his own carver and cut out his way,
To find out right with wrong – it may not be;
And you that do abet him in this kind
Cherish rebellion and are rebels all.

NORTHUMBERLAND
The noble duke hath sworn his coming is
But for his own; and for the right of that
We all have strongly sworn to give him aid;   150
And let him never see joy that breaks that oath!

YORK
Well, well, I see the issue of these arms.
I cannot mend it, I must needs confess,
Because my power is weak and all ill left;   154
But if I could, by him that gave me life,
I would attach you all and make you stoop   156
Unto the sovereign mercy of the king;
But since I cannot, be it known unto you
I do remain as neuter. So fare you well –   159
Unless you please to enter in the castle   160
And there repose you for this night.

BOLINGBROKE
An offer, uncle, that we will accept;
But we must win your grace to go with us
To Bristol Castle, which they say is held
By Bushy, Bagot, and their complices,   165
The caterpillars of the commonwealth,   166
Which I have sworn to weed and pluck away.   167

YORK
It may be I will go with you; but yet I'll pause,
For I am loath to break our country's laws.

---

143 *kind* fashion   154 *all ill left* everything left in disorder   156 *attach* arrest   159 *neuter* neutral   165 *complices* accomplices   166 *caterpillars* i.e., devourers   167 *weed* get rid of

170   Nor friends nor foes, to me welcome you are.
        Things past redress are now with me past care. *Exeunt.*

                              *

∾ **II.4** *Enter Earl of Salisbury and a Welsh Captain.*

WELSH CAPTAIN
        My Lord of Salisbury, we have stayed ten days
2   And hardly kept our countrymen together,
        And yet we hear no tidings from the king.
        Therefore we will disperse ourselves. Farewell.
SALISBURY
        Stay yet another day, thou trusty Welshman.
        The king reposeth all his confidence in thee.
WELSH CAPTAIN
        'Tis thought the king is dead. We will not stay.
8   The bay trees in our country are all withered,
        And meteors fright the fixèd stars of heaven;
10   The pale-faced moon looks bloody on the earth,
11   And lean-looked prophets whisper fearful change;
        Rich men look sad, and ruffians dance and leap –
        The one in fear to lose what they enjoy,
14   The other to enjoy by rage and war.
        These signs forerun the death or fall of kings.
        Farewell. Our countrymen are gone and fled,
17   As well assured Richard their king is dead.   *[Exit.]*
SALISBURY
        Ah, Richard! with the eyes of heavy mind,
        I see thy glory, like a shooting star,
20   Fall to the base earth from the firmament.

        ──────────

170 *Nor . . . are* since I am neutral and view you as neither friends nor foes,
I can welcome you
    II.4 A military camp in Wales **s.d.** *Welsh Captain* (perhaps the famous
Owen Glendower, who is mentioned in III.1.43 and appears in *1 Henry IV*)
2 *hardly* with difficulty   **8–10** *The . . . earth* i.e., earth and the heavens show
omens of disaster   **11** *change* political upheaval   **14** *to enjoy* in hope to gain;
rage violence   **17** *As* as being

Thy sun sets weeping in the lowly west,
Witnessing storms to come, woe, and unrest;   22
Thy friends are fled to wait upon thy foes,   23
And crossly to thy good all fortune goes.   *[Exit.]*   24

                              *

∾ **III.1** *Enter [Bolingbroke] Duke of Hereford, York,*
Northumberland, [Ross, Percy, Willoughby, with]
Bushy and Green prisoners.

BOLINGBROKE
Bring forth these men.
Bushy and Green, I will not vex your souls
(Since presently your souls must part your bodies)   3
With too much urging your pernicious lives,   4
For 'twere no charity; yet, to wash your blood
From off my hands, here in the view of men
I will unfold some causes of your deaths.
You have misled a prince, a royal king,
A happy gentleman in blood and lineaments,
By you unhappied and disfigured clean.   10
You have in manner with your sinful hours   11
Made a divorce betwixt his queen and him,
Broke the possession of a royal bed,
And stained the beauty of a fair queen's cheeks
With tears drawn from her eyes by your foul wrongs.
Myself – a prince by fortune of my birth,
Near to the king in blood, and near in love
Till you did make him misinterpret me –
Have stooped my neck under your injuries
And sighed my English breath in foreign clouds,   20

---

22 *Witnessing* foretelling   23 *wait upon* offer allegiance to   24 *crossly* ad-
versely
   III.1 Before Bristol Castle   3 *presently* immediately; *part* leave   4 *urging*
stressing   10 *clean* completely   11–12 *You have in manner . . . Made a di-*
vorce you have . . . made a kind of divorce   20 *foreign clouds* clouds of breath
exhaled in a foreign land

Eating the bitter bread of banishment,
22 Whilst you have fed upon my signories,
23 Disparked my parks and felled my forest woods,
24 From my own windows torn my household coat,
25 Rased out my imprese, leaving me no sign,
    Save men's opinions and my living blood,
    To show the world I am a gentleman.
    This and much more, much more than twice all this,
    Condemns you to the death. See them delivered over
30 To execution and the hand of death.
BUSHY
    More welcome is the stroke of death to me
    Than Bolingbroke to England. Lords, farewell.
GREEN
    My comfort is that heaven will take our souls
    And plague injustice with the pains of hell.
BOLINGBROKE
    My Lord Northumberland, see them dispatched.
                    [Exeunt Northumberland and others,
                                    with the prisoners.]
    Uncle, you say the queen is at your house.
37 For God's sake, fairly let her be entreated.
38 Tell her I send to her my kind commends;
    Take special care my greetings be delivered.
YORK
40 A gentleman of mine I have dispatched
41 With letters of your love to her at large.
BOLINGBROKE
    Thanks, gentle uncle. Come, lords, away,
43 To fight with Glendower and his complices.
44 A while to work, and after holiday.   *Exeunt.*

                            *

---

22 *signories* domains   23 *Disparked* thrown open to other uses   24 *torn* broken; *coat* coat of arms   25 *Rased out* erased; *imprese* heraldic emblem   37 *entreated* treated   38 *commends* remembrances   41 *at large* conveyed in full   43 *Glendower* (see note at II.4.s.d.)   44 *after* afterwards

∾ **III.2** *[Drums. Flourish and Colors.] Enter the King,
Aumerle, [the Bishop of] Carlisle, etc. [, and Soldiers
and Attendants].*

KING
  Barkloughly Castle call they this at hand?
AUMERLE
  Yea, my lord. How brooks your grace the air   2
  After your late tossing on the breaking seas?
KING
  Needs must I like it well. I weep for joy
  To stand upon my kingdom once again.
  Dear earth, I do salute thee with my hand,
  Though rebels wound thee with their horses' hoofs.
  As a long-parted mother with her child   8
  Plays fondly with her tears and smiles in meeting,   9
  So weeping, smiling, greet I thee, my earth,   10
  And do thee favors with my royal hands.   11
  Feed not thy sovereign's foe, my gentle earth,
  Nor with thy sweets comfort his ravenous sense;   13
  But let thy spiders that suck up thy venom,
  And heavy-gaited toads, lie in their way,   15
  Doing annoyance to the treacherous feet
  Which with usurping steps do trample thee.
  Yield stinging nettles to mine enemies;
  And when they from thy bosom pluck a flower,
  Guard it, I pray thee, with a lurking adder   20
  Whose double tongue may with a mortal touch   21
  Throw death upon thy sovereign's enemies.
  Mock not my senseless conjuration, lords.   23
  This earth shall have a feeling, and these stones

III.2 In front of Barkloughly Castle on the coast of Wales **2** *brooks* enjoys
8 *long-parted mother with* mother long parted from **9** *fondly* dotingly **11**
do . . . hands salute you by touching **13** *sense* appetite **15** *heavy-gaited*
slow-moving **21** *double* forked; *touch* wound **23** *senseless conjuration*
solemn entreaty to things that cannot understand it

25 Prove armèd soldiers ere her native king
Shall falter under foul rebellion's arms.

CARLISLE

Fear not, my lord. That power that made you king
Hath power to keep you king in spite of all.
The means that heavens yield must be embraced
30 And not neglected. Else heaven would,
And we will not. Heavens offer, we refuse
The proffered means of succor and redress.

AUMERLE

He means, my lord, that we are too remiss,
34 Whilst Bolingbroke, through our security,
Grows strong and great in substance and in power.

KING

36 Discomfortable cousin! know'st thou not
37 That when the searching eye of heaven is hid
Behind the globe, that lights the lower world,
Then thieves and robbers range abroad unseen
40 In murders and in outrage boldly here;
But when from under this terrestrial ball
He fires the proud tops of the eastern pines
And darts his light through every guilty hole,
Then murders, treasons, and detested sins,
The cloak of night being plucked from off their backs,
Stand bare and naked, trembling at themselves?
So when this thief, this traitor Bolingbroke,
Who all this while hath reveled in the night
49 Whilst we were wand'ring with the antipodes,
50 Shall see us rising in our throne, the east,
His treasons will sit blushing in his face,
Not able to endure the sight of day,

---

25 *native* legitimate (Richard was born at Bordeaux)   **30–32** *Else . . . redress*
(Carlisle advises that Richard must seize the opportunity heaven offers – i.e.,
to move against Bolingbroke before he knows Richard has returned from Ireland)   **34** *security* overconfidence   **36** *Discomfortable* discouraging   **37–38**
when . . . world when the sun, lighting the other side of the world, is hidden
from view   **49** *Whilst . . . antipodes* while we, like the sun, were with the
people on the other side of the earth

But self-affrighted tremble at his sin.　　　　　　　　53
Not all the water in the rough rude sea
Can wash the balm off from an anointed king.　　　　55
The breath of worldly men cannot depose　　　　　　56
The deputy elected by the Lord.
For every man that Bolingbroke hath pressed　　　　　58
To lift shrewd steel against our golden crown,　　　　59
God for his Richard hath in heavenly pay　　　　　　60
A glorious angel. Then, if angels fight,
Weak men must fall; for heaven still guards the right.
　　Enter Salisbury.
Welcome, my lord. How far off lies your power?　　　63

SALISBURY
Nor near nor farther off, my gracious lord,　　　　　64
Than this weak arm. Discomfort guides my tongue　　65
And bids me speak of nothing but despair.
One day too late, I fear me, noble lord,　　　　　　67
Hath clouded all thy happy days on earth.
O, call back yesterday, bid time return,
And thou shalt have twelve thousand fighting men!　　70
Today, today, unhappy day too late,
O'erthrows thy joys, friends, fortune, and thy state;
For all the Welshmen, hearing thou wert dead,
Are gone to Bolingbroke, dispersed, and fled.

AUMERLE
Comfort, my liege. Why looks your grace so pale?

KING
But now the blood of twenty thousand men　　　　　76
　　Did triumph in my face, and they are fled;
And, till so much blood thither come again,
　　Have I not reason to look pale and dead?
All souls that will be safe, fly from my side;　　　　80
For time hath set a blot upon my pride.

---

53 *self-affrighted* afraid of his own actions　55 *balm* consecrated oil used in
the coronation　56 *worldly* earthly, mortal　58 *pressed* drafted　59 *shrewd*
keen　63 *power* army　64 *near* nearer　65 *Discomfort* discouragement　67–
68 *One . . . earth* i.e., Richard has lived one day longer than his good fortune
76 *But* just; *twenty* (Richard exaggerates Salisbury's *twelve*, l. 70)

AUMERLE

  Comfort, my liege. Remember who you are.

KING

  I had forgot myself. Am I not king?

  Awake, thou coward majesty! thou sleepest.

  Is not the king's name twenty thousand names?

  Arm, arm, my name! A puny subject strikes

  At thy great glory. Look not to the ground,

  Ye favorites of a king. Are we not high?

  High be our thoughts. I know my uncle York

90   Hath power enough to serve our turn. But who comes

    here?

    Enter Scroop.

SCROOP

  More health and happiness betide my liege

  Than can my care-tuned tongue deliver him!

KING

  Mine ear is open and my heart prepared.

94   The worst is worldly loss thou canst unfold.

  Say, is my kingdom lost? Why, 'twas my care;

  And what loss is it to be rid of care?

  Strives Bolingbroke to be as great as we?

  Greater he shall not be; if he serve God,

  We'll serve him too, and be his fellow so.

100   Revolt our subjects? That we cannot mend;

  They break their faith to God as well as us.

  Cry woe, destruction, ruin, and decay:

  The worst is death, and death will have his day.

SCROOP

  Glad am I that your highness is so armed

  To bear the tidings of calamity.

  Like an unseasonable stormy day

  Which makes the silver rivers drown their shores

  As if the world were all dissolved to tears,

109   So high above his limits swells the rage

---

94 *The worst . . . unfold* the worst you can tell me is worldly loss   **109** *his* its (the rage's); *limits* (1) banks, (2) borders

Of Bolingbroke, covering your fearful land   *110*
With hard bright steel, and hearts harder than steel.
Whitebeards have armed their thin and hairless scalps   *112*
Against thy majesty. Boys with women's voices
Strive to speak big, and clap their female joints   *114*
In stiff unwieldy arms against thy crown.
Thy very beadsmen learn to bend their bows   *116*
Of double-fatal yew against thy state.   *117*
Yea, distaff women manage rusty bills   *118*
Against thy seat. Both young and old rebel,   *119*
And all goes worse than I have power to tell.   *120*

KING
Too well, too well thou tell'st a tale so ill.
Where is the Earl of Wiltshire? Where is Bagot?
What is become of Bushy? Where is Green?
That they have let the dangerous enemy
Measure our confines with such peaceful steps?   *125*
If we prevail, their heads shall pay for it.
I warrant they have made peace with Bolingbroke.

SCROOP
Peace have they made with him indeed, my lord.

KING
O villains, vipers, damned without redemption!
Dogs easily won to fawn on any man!   *130*
Snakes in my heartblood warmed that sting my heart!
Three Judases, each one thrice worse than Judas!
Would they make peace? Terrible hell
Make war upon their spotted souls for this!   *134*

SCROOP
Sweet love, I see, changing his property,   *135*
Turns to the sourest and most deadly hate.
Again uncurse their souls. Their peace is made

---

112 *thin* balding   114 *clap* thrust; *female* i.e., small or weak   116 *beadsmen*
old pensioners who pray for their benefactor   117 *double-fatal* poisonous
and used to make war bows   118 *distaff women* spinning women; *manage*
wield; *bills* halberds (heavy, long-handled poleaxes with a pike attached)
119 *seat* throne   125 *Measure our confines* travel from one border to the
other   134 *spotted* stained with treason   135 *property* distinctive quality

138 With heads, and not with hands. Those whom you
          curse
      Have felt the worst of death's destroying wound
140 And lie full low, graved in the hollow ground.
AUMERLE
      Is Bushy, Green, and the Earl of Wiltshire dead?
SCROOP
142 Ay, all of them at Bristow lost their heads.
AUMERLE
      Where is the duke my father with his power?
KING
      No matter where. Of comfort no man speak!
      Let's talk of graves, of worms, and epitaphs,
      Make dust our paper, and with rainy eyes
      Write sorrow on the bosom of the earth.
      Let's choose executors and talk of wills.
      And yet not so – for what can we bequeath,
150 Save our deposèd bodies to the ground?
      Our lands, our lives, and all are Bolingbroke's,
      And nothing can we call our own but death
153 And that small model of the barren earth
154 Which serves as paste and cover to our bones.
      For God's sake let us sit upon the ground
      And tell sad stories of the death of kings!
      How some have been deposed, some slain in war,
158 Some haunted by the ghosts they have deposed,
      Some poisoned by their wives, some sleeping killed –
160 All murdered; for within the hollow crown
      That rounds the mortal temples of a king
162 Keeps death his court; and there the antic sits,
      Scoffing his state and grinning at his pomp;
164 Allowing him a breath, a little scene,

---

138 *with hands* by lifting their hands in surrender   142 *Bristow* (modern
Bristol)   153 *model* (1) part, (2) miniature version   154 *paste and cover* (1)
pastry crust, (2) enclosure   158 *the ghosts . . . deposed* the ghosts of the kings
they have murdered   162 *antic* clown   164–65 *breath . . . monarchize* a
brief time to play the monarch

To monarchize, be feared, and kill with looks;
Infusing him with self and vain conceit,   166
As if this flesh which walls about our life
Were brass impregnable; and humored thus,   168
Comes at the last, and with a little pin   169
Bores through his castle wall, and farewell king!   *170*
Cover your heads, and mock not flesh and blood
With solemn reverence. Throw away respect,
Tradition, form, and ceremonious duty;
For you have but mistook me all this while.
I live with bread like you, feel want, taste grief,
Need friends. Subjected thus,   176
How can you say to me I am a king?

CARLISLE
My lord, wise men ne'er sit and wail their woes,
But presently prevent the ways to wail.   179
To fear the foe, since fear oppresseth strength,   *180*
Gives, in your weakness, strength unto your foe,
And so your follies fight against yourself.
Fear, and be slain – no worse can come to fight;   183
And fight and die is death destroying death,
Where fearing dying pays death servile breath.   185

AUMERLE
My father hath a power. Inquire of him,   186
And learn to make a body of a limb.

KING
Thou chid'st me well. Proud Bolingbroke, I come
To change blows with thee for our day of doom.   189
This ague fit of fear is overblown.   *190*
An easy task it is to win our own.
Say, Scroop, where lies our uncle with his power?

---

166 *self . . . conceit* a puffed-up sense of himself   **168** *humored thus* while the king is thus puffed up   **169** *Comes* death comes   **176** *Subjected thus* subject as I am to these basic human needs   **179** *presently . . . wail* immediately block the paths to grief   **183** *to fight* by fighting   **185** *Where* whereas; *fearing dying* to be afraid to die   **186** *a power* an army; *of* about   **189** *change* exchange; *doom* judgment

Speak sweetly, man, although thy looks be sour.

SCROOP

Men judge by the complexion of the sky

195 The state and inclination of the day;

So may you by my dull and heavy eye:

  My tongue hath but a heavier tale to say.

198 I play the torturer, by small and small

To lengthen out the worst that must be spoken.

200 Your uncle York is joined with Bolingbroke,

And all your northern castles yielded up,

And all your southern gentlemen in arms

Upon his party.

KING   Thou hast said enough.

 [To Aumerle]

204 Beshrew thee, cousin, which didst lead me forth

Of that sweet way I was in to despair!

What say you now? What comfort have we now?

By heaven, I'll hate him everlastingly

That bids me be of comfort any more.

Go to Flint Castle. There I'll pine away;

210 A king, woe's slave, shall kingly woe obey.

That power I have, discharge; and let them go

212 To ear the land that hath some hope to grow,

For I have none. Let no man speak again

To alter this, for counsel is but vain.

AUMERLE

My liege, one word.

KING   He does me double wrong

That wounds me with the flatteries of his tongue.

Discharge my followers. Let them hence away,

From Richard's night to Bolingbroke's fair day.

         [Exeunt.]

*

---

195 *inclination . . . day* trend of the weather **198–99** *by . . . spoken* in breaking the worst news little by little **204** *Beshrew thee* confound you; *forth* out **212** *ear* plow, cultivate

∾ **III.3** *Enter [with Drum and Colors] Bolingbroke,*
    York, Northumberland [, Attendants, and Soldiers].

BOLINGBROKE

So that by this intelligence we learn   1
The Welshmen are dispersed, and Salisbury
Is gone to meet the king, who lately landed
With some few private friends upon this coast.

NORTHUMBERLAND

The news is very fair and good, my lord,   5
Richard not far from hence hath hid his head.

YORK

It would beseem the Lord Northumberland
To say "King Richard." Alack the heavy day
When such a sacred king should hide his head!

NORTHUMBERLAND

Your grace mistakes. Only to be brief,   10
Left I his title out.

YORK   The time hath been,
Would you have been so brief with him, he would
Have been so brief with you to shorten you,   13
For taking so the head, your whole head's length.   14

BOLINGBROKE

Mistake not, uncle, further than you should.

YORK

Take not, good cousin, further than you should,
Lest you mistake the heavens are over our heads.   17

BOLINGBROKE

I know it, uncle, and oppose not myself
Against their will. But who comes here?
    Enter Percy.
Welcome, Harry. What, will not this castle yield?   20

III.3 In front of Flint Castle in Wales **1** *intelligence* news **5–6** *The . . .
head* the news that Richard is in hiding not far away is auspicious and good
13 *to* as to **14** *taking . . . head* thus omitting his title **17** *mistake* ignore the
fact that

PERCY
    The castle royally is manned, my lord,
    Against thy entrance.
BOLINGBROKE
    Royally?
    Why, it contains no king?
PERCY   Yes, my good lord,
    It doth contain a king. King Richard lies
    Within the limits of yon lime and stone;
    And with him are the Lord Aumerle, Lord Salisbury,
    Sir Stephen Scroop, besides a clergyman
    Of holy reverence – who, I cannot learn.
NORTHUMBERLAND
30   O, belike it is the Bishop of Carlisle.
BOLINGBROKE
    Noble lord,
    Go to the rude ribs of that ancient castle;
33   Through brazen trumpet send the breath of parle
    Into his ruined ears, and thus deliver:
    Henry Bolingbroke
    On both his knees doth kiss King Richard's hand
    And sends allegiance and true faith of heart
    To his most royal person; hither come
    Even at his feet to lay my arms and power,
40   Provided that my banishment repealed
    And lands restored again be freely granted.
    If not, I'll use the advantage of my power,
    And lay the summer's dust with show'rs of blood
    Rained from the wounds of slaughtered Englishmen;
    The which, how far off from the mind of Bolingbroke
    It is, such crimson tempest should bedrench
    The fresh green lap of fair King Richard's land,
48   My stooping duty tenderly shall show.
    Go signify as much, while here we march
50   Upon the grassy carpet of this plain.

---

33 *parle* truce   40 *repealed* revoked   48 *stooping duty* submissive kneeling;
tenderly considerately

Let's march without the noise of threat'ning drum,
That from this castle's tottered battlements   52
Our fair appointments may be well perused.   53
Methinks King Richard and myself should meet
With no less terror than the elements
Of fire and water when their thund'ring shock   56
At meeting tears the cloudy cheeks of heaven.
Be he the fire, I'll be the yielding water;
The rage be his, whilst on the earth I rain   59
My waters; on the earth, and not on him.   60
March on, and mark King Richard how he looks.
          The trumpets sound [a parle without, which is then
          answered from within, then a flourish. King] Richard
          appeareth on the walls [with the Bishop of Carlisle,
          Aumerle, Scroop, and Salisbury].
See, see, King Richard doth himself appear,
As doth the blushing discontented sun
From out the fiery portal of the east
When he perceives the envious clouds are bent   65
To dim his glory and to stain the track
Of his bright passage to the occident.   67
YORK
Yet looks he like a king. Behold, his eye,   68
As bright as is the eagle's, lightens forth   69
Controlling majesty. Alack, alack, for woe,   70
That any harm should stain so fair a show!
KING   *[To Northumberland]*
We are amazed; and thus long have we stood   72
To watch the fearful bending of thy knee,
Because we thought ourself thy lawful king.
And if we be, how dare thy joints forget
To pay their awful duty to our presence?   76
If we be not, show us the hand of God

---

52 *tottered* ruined   53 *appointments* equipment   56 *fire and water* lightning
and clouds   59 *rain* (with a pun on "reign"; Q reads "raigne" here)   59–60
I rain . . . him I fall upon the land, not upon him   65 *he* the sun   67 *occi-*
dent west   68 *he* King Richard   69 *lightens forth* flashes out   72 *amazed*
confused, overwhelmed   76 *awful* awed, reverent

78 That hath dismissed us from our stewardship;
For well we know no hand of blood and bone
80 Can gripe the sacred handle of our scepter,
Unless he do profane, steal, or usurp.
And though you think that all, as you have done,
83 Have torn their souls by turning them from us
And we are barren and bereft of friends,
Yet know, my master, God omnipotent,
Is mustering in his clouds on our behalf
Armies of pestilence, and they shall strike
88 Your children yet unborn and unbegot
89 That lift your vassal hands against my head
90 And threat the glory of my precious crown.
Tell Bolingbroke, for yon methinks he stands,
That every stride he makes upon my land
Is dangerous treason. He is come to open
94 The purple testament of bleeding war.
But ere the crown he looks for live in peace,
Ten thousand bloody crowns of mothers' sons
97 Shall ill become the flower of England's face,
Change the complexion of her maid-pale peace
To scarlet indignation, and bedew
100 Her pastor's grass with faithful English blood.
NORTHUMBERLAND
The King of Heaven forbid our lord the king
102 Should so with civil and uncivil arms
Be rushed upon! Thy thrice-noble cousin
Harry Bolingbroke doth humbly kiss thy hand;
And by the honorable tomb he swears
That stands upon your royal grandsire's bones,
And by the royalties of both your bloods
(Currents that spring from one most gracious head),
And by the buried hand of warlike Gaunt,

---

78 *stewardship* management of the country   83 *torn* (1) divided, (2) damned
88–89 *Your . . . That* the children . . . of you who   **89** *vassal* subject   **90**
threat threaten   **94** *purple testament* blood-red will, document   **97** *flower . . .
face* blooming surface of the land   **100** *Her pastor's* her shepherd's (i.e.,
Richard's)   **102** *civil* borne by Englishmen against Englishmen; *uncivil* rude

And by the worth and honor of himself,   *110*
Comprising all that may be sworn or said,
His coming hither hath no further scope
Than for his lineal royalties, and to beg   113
Enfranchisement immediate on his knees;   114
Which on thy royal party granted once,   115
His glittering arms he will commend to rust,   116
His barbèd steeds to stables, and his heart   117
To faithful service of your majesty.
This swears he, as he is a prince and just;
And as I am a gentleman, I credit him.   120

KING
Northumberland, say thus. The king returns: 121
His noble cousin is right welcome hither;
And all the number of his fair demands
Shall be accomplished without contradiction.
With all the gracious utterance thou hast
Speak to his gentle hearing kind commends.   126
    [To Aumerle]
We do debase ourselves, cousin, do we not,
To look so poorly and to speak so fair?
Shall we call back Northumberland and send
Defiance to the traitor, and so die?   *130*

AUMERLE
No, good my lord. Let's fight with gentle words
Till time lend friends, and friends their helpful swords.

KING
O God, O God! that e'er this tongue of mine
That laid the sentence of dread banishment
On yon proud man, should take it off again
With words of sooth! O that I were as great   136
As is my grief, or lesser than my name!   137
Or that I could forget what I have been!

---

113 *lineal royalties* royal birthrights   114 *Enfranchisement* freedom from banishment   115 *on . . . party* on your majesty's part   116 *commend* hand over   117 *barbèd* armored   120 *credit* believe   121 *returns* replies as follows   126 *commends* regards   136 *sooth* flattery   137 *name* title of king

Or not remember what I must be now!
140 Swell'st thou, proud heart? I'll give thee scope to beat,
141 Since foes have scope to beat both thee and me.

AUMERLE
Northumberland comes back from Bolingbroke.

KING
What must the king do now? Must he submit?
The king shall do it. Must he be deposed?
The king shall be contented. Must he lose
146 The name of king? A God's name, let it go!
147 I'll give my jewels for a set of beads,
148 My gorgeous palace for a hermitage,
149 My gay apparel for an almsman's gown,
150 My figured goblets for a dish of wood,
151 My scepter for a palmer's walking staff,
My subjects for a pair of carvèd saints,
And my large kingdom for a little grave,
A little little grave, an obscure grave;
Or I'll be buried in the king's high way,
156 Some way of common trade, where subjects' feet
May hourly trample on their sovereign's head;
For on my heart they tread now whilst I live,
And buried once, why not upon my head?
160 Aumerle, thou weep'st, my tenderhearted cousin!
We'll make foul weather with despisèd tears;
162 Our sighs and they shall lodge the summer corn
163 And make a dearth in this revolting land.
164 Or shall we play the wantons with our woes
And make some pretty match with shedding tears?
As thus – to drop them still upon one place
167 Till they have fretted us a pair of graves
Within the earth; and therein laid – there lies

---

140 *scope* (1) room, (2) permission   141 *scope* (1) opportunity, (2) intention
146 *A* in, of   147 *set of beads* rosary   148 *hermitage* home of a religious
recluse or hermit   149 *an almsman* one living on charity and bound to pray
for his benefactor (hence *beads,* l. 147)   150 *figured* embossed   151 *palmer*
pilgrim   156 *trade* passage   162 *they* tears; *lodge* beat down   163 *revolting*
rebelling   164 *play the wantons* sport   167 *fretted us* washed out for us

Two kinsmen digged their graves with weeping eyes.
Would not this ill do well? Well, well, I see   *170*
I talk but idly, and you laugh at me.
Most mighty prince, my Lord Northumberland,
What says King Bolingbroke? Will his majesty
Give Richard leave to live till Richard die?
You make a leg, and Bolingbroke says ay.   175

NORTHUMBERLAND
My lord, in the base court he doth attend   176
To speak with you, may it please you to come down.

KING
Down, down I come, like glist'ring Phaëthon,   178
Wanting the manage of unruly jades.   179
In the base court? Base court, where kings grow base,   *180*
To come at traitors' calls and do them grace!
In the base court come down? Down court! down king!
For night owls shriek where mounting larks should
    sing.
    [Richard comes down.]

BOLINGBROKE
What says his majesty?

NORTHUMBERLAND   Sorrow and grief of heart
Makes him speak fondly, like a frantic man.   185
Yet he is come.

BOLINGBROKE
Stand all apart
And show fair duty to his majesty.
    He kneels down.
My gracious lord –

KING
Fair cousin, you debase your princely knee   *190*
To make the base earth proud with kissing it.

---

175 *You . . . ay* if you curtsy to him, Bolingbroke will say yes   176 *base court*
lower or outer courtyard; *attend* wait   178 *Phaëthon* (who borrowed the
chariot of his father, Apollo, the sun god, drove it recklessly, nearly set the
world on fire, and was killed)   179 *Wanting . . . of* lacking control over;
jades poor horses   185 *fondly* foolishly; *frantic man* madman

192 Me rather had my heart might feel your love
Than my unpleased eye see your courtesy.
Up, cousin, up! Your heart is up, I know,
Thus high at least, *[Touches his own head.]* although
your knee be low.

BOLINGBROKE *[Rises.]*
My gracious lord, I come but for mine own.

KING
Your own is yours, and I am yours, and all.

BOLINGBROKE
198 So far be mine, my most redoubted lord,
As my true service shall deserve your love.

KING
200 Well you deserve. They well deserve to have
That know the strong'st and surest way to get.
Uncle, give me your hand. Nay, dry your eyes.
203 Tears show their love, but want their remedies.
Cousin, I am too young to be your father,
Though you are old enough to be my heir.
What you will have, I'll give, and willing too;
For do we must what force will have us do.
Set on towards London. Cousin, is it so?

BOLINGBROKE
Yea, my good lord.

KING   Then I must not say no.
[Flourish. Exeunt.]

*

⟶ **III.4** *Enter the Queen with [two Ladies,]*
her Attendants.

QUEEN
What sport shall we devise here in this garden
To drive away the heavy thought of care?

---

192 *Me rather had* I would rather 198 *redoubted* dread 203 *want their*
remedies cannot cure what causes them
   III.4 The Duke of York's garden

LADY
  Madam, we'll play at bowls.   3
QUEEN
  'Twill make me think the world is full of rubs   4
  And that my fortune runs against the bias.   5
LADY
  Madam, we'll dance.
QUEEN
  My legs can keep no measure in delight   7
  When my poor heart no measure keeps in grief.   8
  Therefore no dancing, girl; some other sport.
LADY
  Madam, we'll tell tales.   10
QUEEN
  Of sorrow or of joy?
LADY   Of either, madam.
QUEEN
  Of neither, girl;
  For if of joy, being altogether wanting,
  It doth remember me the more of sorrow;
  Or if of grief, being altogether had,   15
  It adds more sorrow to my want of joy;   16
  For what I have I need not to repeat,
  And what I want it boots not to complain.   18
LADY
  Madam, I'll sing.
QUEEN   'Tis well that thou hast cause;
  But thou shouldst please me better, wouldst thou weep.   20
LADY
  I could weep, madam, would it do you good.
QUEEN
  And I could sing, would weeping do me good,
  And never borrow any tear of thee.

---

3 *bowls* (an early version of bowling, involving a ball and pins, or *rubs*, laid out on a lawn or green)   4 *rubs* impediments (in the game of *bowls*)   5 *bias* curving course (of a bowl)   7 *keep no measure* not keep pace with the steps of a stately dance   8 *no measure keeps* knows no limit   15 *had* experienced by me 16 *want* lack   18 *boots* helps

Enter Gardeners [one the Master, the other two his Men].
But stay, here come the gardeners.
Let's step into the shadow of these trees.
26 My wretchedness unto a row of pins,
27 They will talk of state, for every one doth so
28 Against a change. Woe is forerun with woe.
[Queen and Ladies step aside.]

GARDENER
Go bind thou up young dangling apricots,
30 Which, like unruly children, make their sire
31 Stoop with oppression of their prodigal weight.
Give some supportance to the bending twigs.
Go thou and, like an executioner,
Cut off the heads of too-fast-growing sprays
That look too lofty in our commonwealth.
36 All must be even in our government.
You thus employed, I will go root away
The noisome weeds which without profit suck
The soil's fertility from wholesome flowers.

FIRST MAN
40 Why should we, in the compass of a pale,
Keep law and form and due proportion,
Showing, as in a model, our firm estate,
When our sea-wallèd garden, the whole land,
Is full of weeds, her fairest flowers choked up,
Her fruit trees all unpruned, her hedges ruined,
46 Her knots disordered, and her wholesome herbs
Swarming with caterpillars?

GARDENER   Hold thy peace.
He that hath suffered this disordered spring
Hath now himself met with the fall of leaf.
50 The weeds which his broad-spreading leaves did
    shelter,
51 That seemed in eating him to hold him up,

---

26 *My . . . pins* i.e., I would bet my grief against a trifle   27 *state* politics
28 *Against* just before; *forerun with* foreshadowed by   31 *prodigal* excessive
36 *even* equal   40 *a pale* an enclosed garden   46 *knots* flower beds laid out
in patterns   51 *in* while

Are plucked up root and all by Bolingbroke –
I mean the Earl of Wiltshire, Bushy, Green.

SECOND MAN

What, are they dead?

GARDENER   They are; and Bolingbroke
Hath seized the wasteful king. O, what pity is it
That he had not so trimmed and dressed his land
As we this garden! We at time of year   57
Do wound the bark, the skin of our fruit trees,
Lest, being overproud in sap and blood,   59
With too much riches it confound itself.   60
Had he done so to great and growing men,
They might have lived to bear, and he to taste
Their fruits of duty. Superfluous branches
We lop away, that bearing boughs may live.   64
Had he done so, himself had borne the crown,
Which waste of idle hours hath quite thrown down.

SECOND MAN

What, think you the king shall be deposed?

GARDENER

Depressed he is already, and deposed   68
'Tis doubt he will be. Letters came last night   69
To a dear friend of the good Duke of York's   70
That tell black tidings.

QUEEN

O, I am pressed to death through want of speaking!   72
[Comes forward.]
Thou old Adam's likeness, set to dress this garden,   73
How dares thy harsh rude tongue sound this unpleas-
ing news?
What Eve, what serpent, hath suggested thee   75

---

57 *at . . . year* in season   59 *overproud in* swollen with   60 *confound* destroy
64 *bearing* fruit-bearing   68 *Depressed* brought low   69 *'Tis doubt* there is
fear   72 *pressed to death* tortured as by a heavy weight crushing me (perhaps
a reference to the practice by which those who refused to plead guilty or innocent to a criminal charge were literally pressed with weights to force a plea
and sometimes died)   73 *old Adam* the first gardener   75 *suggested* tempted

To make a second fall of cursèd man?
Why dost thou say King Richard is deposed?
Dar'st thou, thou little better thing than earth,

79   Divine his downfall? Say, where, when, and how
80   Cam'st thou by this ill tidings? Speak, thou wretch!

GARDENER
Pardon me, madam. Little joy have I

82   To breathe this news; yet what I say is true.
King Richard, he is in the mighty hold
Of Bolingbroke. Their fortunes both are weighed.
In your lord's scale is nothing but himself,
And some few vanities that make him light;
But in the balance of great Bolingbroke,
Besides himself, are all the English peers,

89   And with that odds he weighs King Richard down.
90   Post you to London, and you will find it so.
I speak no more than every one doth know.

QUEEN
Nimble mischance, that art so light of foot,

93   Doth not thy embassage belong to me,
And am I last that knows it? O, thou thinkest
To serve me last, that I may longest keep

96   Thy sorrow in my breast. Come, ladies, go
To meet at London London's king in woe.
What, was I born to this, that my sad look

99   Should grace the triumph of great Bolingbroke?
100   Gardener, for telling me these news of woe,
Pray God the plants thou graft'st may never grow.

                             Exit [with Ladies].

GARDENER
Poor queen, so that thy state might be no worse,
I would my skill were subject to thy curse!

104   Here did she fall a tear; here in this place

---

79 *Divine* prophesy by occult means   82 *To breathe* in speaking   89 *odds* advantage   90 *Post you* ride quickly   93 *embassage* message   96 *Thy sorrow* the sorrow you report   99 *triumph* triumphal procession   104 *fall* drop

I'll set a bank of rue, sour herb of grace.   105
Rue, even for ruth, here shortly shall be seen,   106
In the remembrance of a weeping queen.   *Exeunt.*

                              ✳

∾ **IV.1** *Enter Bolingbroke, with the Lords [Aumerle,*
    Northumberland, Percy, Fitzwater, Surrey, and
    another Lord, with Bishop of Carlisle, Abbot of
    Westminster, Attendants, and Herald] to Parliament.

BOLINGBROKE
    Call forth Bagot.
        Enter [Officers with] Bagot.
    Now, Bagot, freely speak thy mind,
    What thou dost know of noble Gloucester's death;
    Who wrought it with the king, and who performed   4
    The bloody office of his timeless end.   5
BAGOT
    Then set before my face the Lord Aumerle.
BOLINGBROKE
    Cousin, stand forth, and look upon that man.
BAGOT
    My Lord Aumerle, I know your daring tongue
    Scorns to unsay what once it hath delivered.
    In that dead time when Gloucester's death was plotted,   10
    I heard you say "Is not my arm of length,   11
    That reacheth from the restful English court   12
    As far as Calais to mine uncle's head?"
    Amongst much other talk that very time
    I heard you say that you had rather refuse
    The offer of an hundred thousand crowns

---

105 *grace* repentance **106** *ruth* pity

IV.1 Westminster Hall **4** *wrought . . . king* (1) worked upon the king to
convince him to have Gloucester murdered, (2) worked with the king on the
murder **5** *office* job; *timeless* untimely **10** *dead* dark, silent **11** *of length*
long **12** *restful* calm, untroubled by Gloucester

17   Than Bolingbroke's return to England;

18   Adding withal, how blessed this land would be

19   In this your cousin's death.

AUMERLE   Princes and noble lords,

20   What answer shall I make to this base man?

21   Shall I so much dishonor my fair stars

22   On equal terms to give him chastisement?

     Either I must, or have mine honor soiled

24   With the attainder of his slanderous lips.

25   There is my gage, the manual seal of death

     That marks thee out for hell. I say thou liest,

     And will maintain what thou hast said is false

28   In thy heartblood, though being all too base

29   To stain the temper of my knightly sword.

BOLINGBROKE

30   Bagot, forbear; thou shalt not take it up.

AUMERLE

31   Excepting one, I would he were the best

32   In all this presence that hath moved me so.

FITZWATER

33   If that thy valor stand on sympathy,

     There is my gage, Aumerle, in gage to thine.

     By that fair sun which shows me where thou stand'st,

36   I heard thee say, and vauntingly thou spak'st it,

     That thou wert cause of noble Gloucester's death.

     If thou deniest it twenty times, thou liest,

     And I will turn thy falsehood to thy heart,

40   Where it was forgèd, with my rapier's point.

AUMERLE

     Thou dar'st not, coward, live to see that day.

---

17 *Than . . . return* than have Bolingbroke return   18 *withal* besides   19 *this your cousin's* Bolingbroke's   21 *fair stars* high rank and fortune   22 *On . . . chastisement* as to fight him as my equal in rank   24 *attainder* disgraceful accusation   25 *the manual . . . death* your death warrant sealed by my hand   28 *being* it is   29 *temper* well-honed steel   31 *one* i.e., Bolingbroke   32 *presence* present company; *moved* angered   33 *If . . . sympathy* if your valor can show itself only on those who are your equals in blood   36 *vauntingly* boastfully   40 *forgèd* crafted

FITZWATER
  Now, by my soul, I would it were this hour.
AUMERLE
  Fitzwater, thou art damned to hell for this.
PERCY
  Aumerle, thou liest. His honor is as true
  In this appeal as thou art all unjust;   45
  And that thou art so, there I throw my gage
  To prove it on thee to the extremest point   47
  Of mortal breathing. Seize it if thou dar'st.
AUMERLE
  And if I do not, may my hands rot off
  And never brandish more revengeful steel   50
  Over the glittering helmet of my foe!
ANOTHER LORD
  I task the earth to the like, forsworn Aumerle;   52
  And spur thee on with full as many lies   53
  As may be hollowed in thy treacherous ear   54
  From sun to sun. There is my honor's pawn.   55
  Engage it to the trial, if thou darest.   56
AUMERLE
  Who sets me else? By heaven, I'll throw at all!   57
  I have a thousand spirits in one breast
  To answer twenty thousand such as you.
SURREY
  My Lord Fitzwater, I do remember well   60
  The very time Aumerle and you did talk.
FITZWATER
  'Tis very true. You were in presence then,   62
  And you can witness with me this is true.
SURREY
  As false, by heaven, as heaven itself is true!

---

45 *appeal* accusation; *all unjust* completely false   47–48 *to . . . breathing*
even if I have to go as far as dying or killing   52 *task . . . like* burden the
ground with another gage   53 *lies* accusations of lying   54 *hollowed* loudly
shouted   55 *pawn* pledge   56 *Engage . . . trial* take it as a challenge to fight
57 *sets me* puts up stakes against me; *throw at all* throw down gloves against
you all   62 *in presence* present at court

FITZWATER
　Surrey, thou liest.
SURREY　　　　　　Dishonorable boy!
　That lie shall lie so heavy on my sword
　That it shall render vengeance and revenge
　Till thou the lie giver and that lie do lie
　In earth as quiet as thy father's skull.
70　In proof whereof there is my honor's pawn.
　Engage it to the trial if thou dar'st.
FITZWATER
72　How fondly dost thou spur a forward horse!
　If I dare eat, or drink, or breathe, or live,
74　I dare meet Surrey in a wilderness,
　And spit upon him whilst I say he lies,
　And lies, and lies. There is my bond of faith
77　To tie thee to my strong correction.
78　As I intend to thrive in this new world,
79　Aumerle is guilty of my true appeal.
80　Besides, I heard the banished Norfolk say
　That thou, Aumerle, didst send two of thy men
　To execute the noble duke at Calais.
AUMERLE
　Some honest Christian trust me with a gage
84　That Norfolk lies. Here do I throw down this,
85　If he may be repealed to try his honor.
BOLINGBROKE
86　These differences shall all rest under gage
　Till Norfolk be repealed. Repealed he shall be
　And, though mine enemy, restored again
　To all his lands and signories. When he is returned,
90　Against Aumerle we will enforce his trial.

---

72 *fondly* foolishly; *forward* willing　74 *in a wilderness* i.e., where there would be no help and no escape　77 *correction* punishment　78 *in . . . world* under the new king　79 *appeal* accusation　84 *this* i.e., gage or glove (although Aumerle has just asked to borrow a *gage,* he has thrown down only one, at l. 25, so he should have one of his own left here)　85 *repealed* called back; *try* put to the test　86 *under gage* as challenges

CARLISLE
    That honorable day shall never be seen.
    Many a time hath banished Norfolk fought
    For Jesu Christ in glorious Christian field,
    Streaming the ensign of the Christian cross   94
    Against black pagans, Turks, and Saracens;   95
    And, toiled with works of war, retired himself   96
    To Italy; and there, at Venice, gave
    His body to that pleasant country's earth
    And his pure soul unto his captain, Christ,
    Under whose colors he had fought so long.   100
BOLINGBROKE
    Why, bishop, is Norfolk dead?
CARLISLE
    As surely as I live, my lord.
BOLINGBROKE
    Sweet peace conduct his sweet soul to the bosom   103
    Of good old Abraham! Lords appellants,   104
    Your differences shall all rest under gage
    Till we assign you to your days of trial.
        Enter York [attended].
YORK
    Great Duke of Lancaster, I come to thee
    From plume-plucked Richard, who with willing soul   108
    Adopts thee heir and his high scepter yields
    To the possession of thy royal hand.   *110*
    Ascend his throne, descending now from him,
    And long live Henry, fourth of that name!
BOLINGBROKE
    In God's name I'll ascend the regal throne.
CARLISLE
    Marry, God forbid!

---

94 *Streaming* flying; *ensign* banner   95 *black pagans* evil unbelievers (in
Christianity); *Saracens* Muslims   96 *toiled* worn out   100 *colors* flag 103–
4 *the bosom . . . Abraham* heavenly rest   104 *appellants* who have made
charges against one another   108 *plume-plucked* stripped of ornament, pathetic

115 Worst in this royal presence may I speak,
    Yet, best beseeming me to speak the truth:
    Would God that any in this noble presence
    Were enough noble to be upright judge
119 Of noble Richard! then true noblesse would
120 Learn him forbearance from so foul a wrong.
    What subject can give sentence on his king?
    And who sits here that is not Richard's subject?
123 Thieves are not judged but they are by to hear,
    Although apparent guilt be seen in them;
    And shall the figure of God's majesty,
    His captain, steward, deputy elect,
    Anointed, crownèd, planted many years,
    Be judged by subject and inferior breath,
129 And he himself not present? O, forfend it God
130 That, in a Christian climate, souls refined
131 Should show so heinous, black, obscene a deed!
    I speak to subjects, and a subject speaks,
    Stirred up by God, thus boldly for his king.
    My Lord of Hereford here, whom you call king,
    Is a foul traitor to proud Hereford's king;
    And if you crown him, let me prophesy,
137 The blood of English shall manure the ground
    And future ages groan for this foul act;
    Peace shall go sleep with Turks and infidels,
140 And in this seat of peace tumultuous wars
141 Shall kin with kin and kind with kind confound;
    Disorder, horror, fear, and mutiny
    Shall here inhabit, and this land be called
144 The field of Golgotha and dead men's skulls.

115–16 *Worst . . . truth* though I may seem the least worthy speaker in such royal company, yet it falls upon me, as a clergyman, to speak the truth   **119** *noblesse* nobility   **123** *but* unless; *by* present   **129** *forfend* forbid   **130** *souls refined* civilized people   **131** *obscene* ill-omened, unlucky   **137** *English* Englishmen; *manure* fertilize   **141** *kin* kinsmen; *kind* fellow countrymen; *confound* destroy   **144** *Golgotha* Calvary, outside Jerusalem, where Jesus was crucified, and which was known as the "place of skulls" (Mark 15:22)

O, if you raise this house against this house,
It will the woefullest division prove
That ever fell upon this cursèd earth.
Prevent it, resist it, let it not be so,
Lest child, child's children cry against you woe.

NORTHUMBERLAND
Well have you argued, sir; and for your pains   *150*
Of capital treason we arrest you here.   151
My Lord of Westminster, be it your charge
To keep him safely till his day of trial.
[May it please you, lords, to grant the commons' suit?   154

BOLINGBROKE
Fetch hither Richard, that in common view
He may surrender. So we shall proceed
Without suspicion.   157

YORK   I will be his conduct.   *Exit.*

BOLINGBROKE
Lords, you that here are under our arrest,
Procure your sureties for your days of answer.   159
Little are we beholding to your love,   *160*
And little looked for at your helping hands.
    *Enter Richard and York [with Officers bearing the
    crown, etc.].*

RICHARD
Alack, why am I sent for to a king
Before I have shook off the regal thoughts
Wherewith I reigned? I hardly yet have learned
To insinuate, flatter, bow, and bend my knee.
Give sorrow leave a while to tutor me
To this submission. Yet I well remember
The favors of these men. Were they not mine?   168
Did they not sometime cry "All hail!" to me?

---

151 *Of* on the charge of; *capital* carrying the death penalty **154–318** (these
lines are interpolated from the folio text; see Note on the Text)   **154** *suit* request for formal parliamentary proceedings against Richard   **157** *conduct* escort   **159** *sureties* men who will be responsible for your appearance   **168**
favors faces and friendly acts

170   So Judas did to Christ; but he, in twelve,
        Found truth in all but one; I, in twelve thousand none.
        God save the king! Will no man say amen?
173   Am I both priest and clerk? Well then, amen!
        God save the king! although I be not he;
        And yet amen, if heaven do think him me.
        To do what service am I sent for hither?

YORK

        To do that office of thine own good will
178   Which tired majesty did make thee offer –
        The resignation of thy state and crown
180   To Henry Bolingbroke.

RICHARD

        Give me the crown. Here, cousin, seize the crown.
        Here, cousin,
        On this side my hand, and on that side thine.
        Now is this golden crown like a deep well
185   That owes two buckets, filling one another,
        The emptier ever dancing in the air,
        The other down, unseen, and full of water.
        That bucket down and full of tears am I,
        Drinking my griefs whilst you mount up on high.

BOLINGBROKE

190   I thought you had been willing to resign.

RICHARD

        My crown I am, but still my griefs are mine.
        You may my glories and my state depose,
        But not my griefs. Still am I king of those.

BOLINGBROKE

        Part of your cares you give me with your crown.

RICHARD

        Your cares set up do not pluck my cares down.
196   My care is loss of care, by old care done;

---

173 *Am . . . clerk* must I pray like the priest and say amen like the clerk   **178**
tired majesty weariness of kingship   **185** *owes* owns, has   **196, 197** *care* (1)
grief, worry, (2) responsibility, (3) concern, careful attention

Your care is gain of care, by new care won.
The cares I give I have, though given away;
They tend the crown, yet still with me they stay.   199
BOLINGBROKE
Are you contented to resign the crown?   200
RICHARD
Ay, no; no, ay; for I must nothing be;   201
Therefore no no, for I resign to thee.
Now mark me how I will undo myself.   203
I give this heavy weight from off my head
And this unwieldy scepter from my hand,
The pride of kingly sway from out my heart.
With mine own tears I wash away my balm,
With mine own hands I give away my crown,
With mine own tongue deny my sacred state,
With mine own breath release all duteous oaths.   210
All pomp and majesty I do forswear;
My manors, rents, revenues I forgo;
My acts, decrees, and statutes I deny.
God pardon all oaths that are broke to me!
God keep all vows unbroke are made to thee!
Make me, that nothing have, with nothing grieved,
And thou with all pleased, that hast all achieved!
Long mayst thou live in Richard's seat to sit,
And soon lie Richard in an earthy pit!
God save King Henry, unkinged Richard says,   220
And send him many years of sunshine days!
What more remains?
NORTHUMBERLAND   No more, but that you read
These accusations and these grievous crimes
Committed by your person and your followers
Against the state and profit of this land,   225
That, by confessing them, the souls of men

---

199 *tend* attend, go with   201 *Ay . . . ay* (1) yes, no; no, yes, (2) I, no; no, I
203 *undo* strip and ruin   225 *state and profit* order and prosperity

227   May deem that you are worthily deposed.
RICHARD
228   Must I do so? and must I ravel out
       My weaved-up follies? Gentle Northumberland,
230   If thy offenses were upon record,
231   Would it not shame thee in so fair a troop
232   To read a lecture of them? If thou wouldst,
       There shouldst thou find one heinous article,
       Containing the deposing of a king
235   And cracking the strong warrant of an oath,
       Marked with a blot, damned in the book of heaven.
       Nay, all of you that stand and look upon me
238   Whilst that my wretchedness doth bait myself,
       Though some of you, with Pilate, wash your hands,
240   Showing an outward pity, yet you Pilates
241   Have here delivered me to my sour cross,
       And water cannot wash away your sin.
NORTHUMBERLAND
243   My lord, dispatch. Read o'er these articles.
RICHARD
       Mine eyes are full of tears; I cannot see.
       And yet salt water blinds them not so much
246   But they can see a sort of traitors here.
       Nay, if I turn mine eyes upon myself,
       I find myself a traitor with the rest;
       For I have given here my soul's consent
250   T' undeck the pompous body of a king;
       Made glory base, a sovereignty a slave,
252   Proud majesty a subject, state a peasant.
NORTHUMBERLAND
       My lord –
RICHARD
254   No lord of thine, thou haught, insulting man,

---

227 *worthily* justly 228 *ravel out* unravel 231 *fair a troop* large and noble
a crowd 232 *read . . . them* read them aloud and in public 235 *an oath*
i.e., your oath of allegiance to me 238 *bait* torment 241 *sour* bitter 243
dispatch make haste 246 *sort* gang 250 *pompous* full of pomp and cere-
mony, stately 252 *state* magnificence, power 254 *haught* arrogant

Nor no man's lord. I have no name, no title –
No, not that name was given me at the font –   256
But 'tis usurped. Alack the heavy day,
That I have worn so many winters out
And know not now what name to call myself!
O that I were a mockery king of snow,   260
Standing before the sun of Bolingbroke
To melt myself away in water drops!
Good king, great king, and yet not greatly good,
An if my word be sterling yet in England,   264
Let it command a mirror hither straight,
That it may show me what a face I have
Since it is bankrupt of his majesty.

BOLINGBROKE
Go some of you and fetch a looking glass.

          [Exit an Attendant.]

NORTHUMBERLAND
Read o'er this paper while the glass doth come.

RICHARD
Fiend, thou torments me ere I come to hell!   270

BOLINGBROKE
Urge it no more, my Lord Northumberland.

NORTHUMBERLAND
The commons will not then be satisfied.

RICHARD
They shall be satisfied. I'll read enough
When I do see the very book indeed
Where all my sins are writ, and that's myself.

    Enter one with a glass.

Give me that glass, and therein will I read.
No deeper wrinkles yet? Hath sorrow struck
So many blows upon this face of mine
And made no deeper wounds? O flattering glass,
Like to my followers in prosperity,   280

256–57 *No . . . usurped* i.e., even Richard, the name given me at the baptismal font, has been threatened (perhaps by the rumor that he was illegitimate)   **264** *An if* if; *sterling* valid currency

Thou dost beguile me! Was this face the face
That every day under his household roof
Did keep ten thousand men? Was this the face
284 That like the sun did make beholders wink?
285 Is this the face which faced so many follies
That was at last outfaced by Bolingbroke?
A brittle glory shineth in this face.
As brittle as the glory is the face,
    [Dashes the glass to the floor.]
289 For there it is, cracked in a hundred shivers.
290 Mark, silent king, the moral of this sport –
How soon my sorrow hath destroyed my face.

BOLINGBROKE

292 The shadow of your sorrow hath destroyed
The shadow of your face.

RICHARD   Say that again.
The shadow of my sorrow? Ha! let's see!
'Tis very true; my grief lies all within;
And these external manners of laments
Are merely shadows to the unseen grief
That swells with silence in the tortured soul.
There lies the substance; and I thank thee, king,
300 For thy great bounty that not only giv'st
Me cause to wail, but teachest me the way
302 How to lament the cause. I'll beg one boon,
And then be gone and trouble you no more.
Shall I obtain it?

BOLINGBROKE   Name it, fair cousin.

RICHARD

Fair cousin? I am greater than a king;
For when I was a king, my flatterers
Were then but subjects; being now a subject,
308 I have a king here to my flatterer.

---

284 *wink* close their eyes   285 *faced* (1) countenanced, (2) permitted   289
shivers shards   292–93 *shadow . . . shadow* outward show . . . reflection
300 *that* who   302 *boon* favor   308 *to* as

Being so great, I have no need to beg.

BOLINGBROKE
Yet ask.   310

RICHARD
And shall I have?

BOLINGBROKE
You shall.

RICHARD
Then give me leave to go.

BOLINGBROKE
Whither?

RICHARD
Whither you will, so I were from your sights.

BOLINGBROKE
Go some of you, convey him to the Tower.   316

RICHARD
O, good! Convey? Conveyers are you all,   317
That rise thus nimbly by a true king's fall.]
          [Exit Richard, with some Lords and a Guard.]

BOLINGBROKE
On Wednesday next we solemnly proclaim
Our coronation. Lords, be ready all.   320
                                              Exeunt.
               Manent [the Abbot of] Westminster,
                  [the Bishop of] Carlisle, Aumerle.

ABBOT
A woeful pageant have we here beheld.

CARLISLE
The woe's to come. The children yet unborn
Shall feel this day as sharp to them as thorn.

AUMERLE
You holy clergymen, is there no plot
To rid the realm of this pernicious blot?

ABBOT
My lord,
Before I freely speak my mind herein,

---

316 *convey* escort   **317** *Convey* (slang for "steal")

328 You shall not only take the sacrament
To bury mine intents, but also to effect
330 Whatever I shall happen to devise.
I see your brows are full of discontent,
Your hearts of sorrow, and your eyes of tears.
Come home with me to supper. I will lay
A plot shall show us all a merry day.   *Exeunt.*

*

∾ **V.1** *Enter the Queen with [Ladies,] her Attendants.*

QUEEN
This way the king will come. This is the way
2 To Julius Caesar's ill-erected tower,
To whose flint bosom my condemnèd lord
Is doomed a prisoner by proud Bolingbroke.
Here let us rest, if this rebellious earth
6 Have any resting for her true king's queen.
    Enter Richard [and Guard].
But soft, but see, or rather do not see,
My fair rose wither. Yet look up, behold,
That you in pity may dissolve to dew
10 And wash him fresh again with true-love tears.
11 Ah, thou the model where old Troy did stand,
12 Thou map of honor, thou King Richard's tomb,
13 And not King Richard! Thou most beauteous inn,
Why should hard-favored grief be lodged in thee
When triumph is become an alehouse guest?
RICHARD
Join not with grief, fair woman, do not so,
To make my end too sudden. Learn, good soul,

328–30 *take . . . devise* receive the sacrament of Communion as a pledge that
you will both hide my plans and help me carry them out
    V.1 A London street leading to the Tower   **2** *Julius Caesar's . . . tower* i.e.,
the Tower of London, a prison; *ill-erected* erected with unfortunate results
6 *Have . . . resting* can offer a resting place   **11** *model . . . stand* ground plan
of ruin, like that of Troy after its fall   **12** *map* pattern   **13–15** *inn . . . alehouse* hotel (Richard) . . . cheapest kind of pub or tavern (Bolingbroke)

To think our former state a happy dream;
From which awaked, the truth of what we are
Shows us but this. I am sworn brother, sweet,   *20*
To grim Necessity, and he and I
Will keep a league till death. Hie thee to France   *22*
And cloister thee in some religious house.
Our holy lives must win a new world's crown,   *24*
Which our profane hours here have thrown down.   *25*

QUEEN
What, is my Richard both in shape and mind
Transformed and weakened? Hath Bolingbroke de-
    posed
Thine intellect? Hath he been in thy heart?
The lion dying thrusteth forth his paw
And wounds the earth, if nothing else, with rage   *30*
To be o'erpowered; and wilt thou pupil-like   *31*
Take the correction mildly, kiss the rod,   *32*
And fawn on rage with base humility,
Which art a lion and the king of beasts?

RICHARD
A king of beasts indeed! If aught but beasts,
I had been still a happy king of men.
Good sometimes queen, prepare thee hence for France.
Think I am dead, and that even here thou takest,
As from my deathbed, thy last living leave.
In winter's tedious nights sit by the fire   *40*
With good old folks, and let them tell thee tales   *41*
Of woeful ages long ago betid;
And ere thou bid good night, to quite their griefs   *43*
Tell thou the lamentable tale of me,
And send the hearers weeping to their beds.
For why, the senseless brands will sympathize   *46*
The heavy accent of thy moving tongue

---

22 *keep a league* maintain an alliance; *Hie thee* take yourself   24 *new world's*
heavenly   25 *thrown* (two syllables)   31 *To be* at being   32 *kiss the rod* (a
proverbial expression for submissiveness)   41–42 *tales . . . betid* tales of woe
that happened in ages long past   43 *quite* requite; *griefs* tales of woe   46 *For
why* because; *senseless brands* inanimate kindling; *sympathize* respond to

And in compassion weep the fire out;
And some will mourn in ashes, some coal-black,
50   For the deposing of a rightful king.
       Enter Northumberland [attended].
NORTHUMBERLAND
My lord, the mind of Bolingbroke is changed.
52   You must to Pomfret, not unto the Tower.
And, madam, there is order ta'en for you:
With all swift speed you must away to France.
RICHARD
55   Northumberland, thou ladder wherewithal
The mounting Bolingbroke ascends my throne,
The time shall not be many hours of age
58   More than it is, ere foul sin gathering head
Shall break into corruption. Thou shalt think,
60   Though he divide the realm and give thee half,
61   It is too little, helping him to all.
He shall think that thou, which knowest the way
To plant unrightful kings, wilt know again,
Being ne'er so little urged another way,
65   To pluck him headlong from the usurped throne.
66   The love of wicked men converts to fear;
That fear to hate, and hate turns one or both
68   To worthy danger and deservèd death.
NORTHUMBERLAND
My guilt be on my head, and there an end!
70   Take leave and part, for you must part forthwith.
RICHARD
Doubly divorced! Bad men, you violate
A twofold marriage – 'twixt my crown and me,
And then betwixt me and my married wife.
Let me unkiss the oath 'twixt thee and me;
And yet not so, for with a kiss 'twas made.

---

52 *Pomfret* Pontefract Castle in Yorkshire (the scene of V.5), sometimes pro-
nounced "Pumfret" or written Pomfret, as here   55 *wherewithal* by means of
which   58 *gathering head* coming to a head, like a boil or pimple   61 *helping him* since you helped him   65 *To* how to   66 *converts* changes   68 *worthy* merited   70 *part . . . part* separate . . . depart

Part us, Northumberland – I towards the north,
Where shivering cold and sickness pines the clime;   77
My wife to France, from whence, set forth in pomp,
She came adornèd hither like sweet May,
Sent back like Hallowmas or short'st of day.   80

QUEEN
And must we be divided? Must we part?

RICHARD
Ay, hand from hand, my love, and heart from heart.

QUEEN
Banish us both, and send the king with me.

NORTHUMBERLAND
That were some love, but little policy.   84

QUEEN
Then whither he goes, thither let me go.

RICHARD
So two, together weeping, make one woe.   86
Weep thou for me in France, I for thee here.
Better far off than near, but ne'er the near.   88
Go, count thy way with sighs; I mine with groans.

QUEEN
So longest way shall have the longest moans.   90

RICHARD
Twice for one step I'll groan, the way being short,
And piece the way out with a heavy heart.   92
Come, come, in wooing sorrow let's be brief,
Since, wedding it, there is such length in grief.
One kiss shall stop our mouths, and dumbly part.   95
Thus give I mine, and thus take I thy heart.

QUEEN
Give me mine own again. 'Twere no good part
To take on me to keep and kill thy heart.
So, now I have mine own again, be gone,

---

77 *pines the clime* make the climate an enfeebling one   80 *Hallowmas* All
Saints' Day (November 1); *short'st of day* the winter solstice   84 *policy* political wisdom   86 *So* no, for thus   88 *near . . . near* being near, never be
nearer   92 *piece . . . out* lengthen the trip   95 *dumbly* silently

100   That I may strive to kill it with a groan.
RICHARD
101   We make woe wanton with this fond delay.
         Once more adieu! The rest let sorrow say.   *Exeunt.*

                              *

∾ **V.2** *Enter Duke of York and the Duchess.*

DUCHESS
         My lord, you told me you would tell the rest,
         When weeping made you break the story off
         Of our two cousins coming into London.
YORK
4   Where did I leave?
DUCHESS   At that sad stop, my lord,
5   Where rude misgoverned hands from windows' tops
         Threw dust and rubbish on King Richard's head.
YORK
         Then, as I said, the duke, great Bolingbroke,
         Mounted upon a hot and fiery steed
9   Which his aspiring rider seemed to know,
10   With slow but stately pace kept on his course,
         Whilst all tongues cried, "God save thee, Bolingbroke!"
         You would have thought the very windows spake,
         So many greedy looks of young and old
         Through casements darted their desiring eyes
         Upon his visage; and that all the walls
16   With painted imagery had said at once,
         "Jesu preserve thee! Welcome, Bolingbroke!"
         Whilst he, from the one side to the other turning,
         Bareheaded, lower than his proud steed's neck,
20   Bespake them thus, "I thank you, countrymen."
         And thus still doing, thus he passed along.

---

101 *wanton* careless; *fond* (1) foolish, (2) affectionate
V.2 Duke of York's house   4 *leave* leave off   5 *misgoverned* unruly; *windows' tops* upper windows   9 *Which . . . know* which seemed to know its ambitious rider   16 *With . . . imagery* painted with figures like a tapestry

DUCHESS

    Alack, poor Richard! Where rode he the whilst?

YORK

    As in a theater the eyes of men,

    After a well-graced actor leaves the stage,   24

    Are idly bent on him that enters next,   25

    Thinking his prattle to be tedious,

    Even so, or with much more contempt, men's eyes

    Did scowl on gentle Richard. No man cried, "God save

       him!"

    No joyful tongue gave him his welcome home,

    But dust was thrown upon his sacred head;   30

    Which with such gentle sorrow he shook off,

    His face still combating with tears and smiles,

    The badges of his grief and patience,   33

    That, had not God for some strong purpose steeled

    The hearts of men, they must perforce have melted

    And barbarism itself have pitied him.   36

    But heaven hath a hand in these events,

    To whose high will we bound our calm contents.   38

    To Bolingbroke are we sworn subjects now,

    Whose state and honor I for aye allow.   40

       [Enter Aumerle.]

DUCHESS

    Here comes my son Aumerle.

YORK   Aumerle that was;

    But that is lost for being Richard's friend,   42

    And, madam, you must call him Rutland now.

    I am in parliament pledge for his truth

    And lasting fealty to the new-made king.   45

DUCHESS

    Welcome, my son. Who are the violets now   46

    That strew the green lap of the new-come spring?

—————

24 *well-graced* (1) graceful, (2) well received   25 *idly* listlessly   33 *badges* tokens   36 *barbarism itself* even savages   38 *To . . . contents* we limit our wishes to calm content with heaven's high will   40 *state* high rank; *for aye allow* forever accept   42 *that* that title   45 *fealty* loyalty   46–47 *Who . . . spring* i.e., who are the new king's favorites

AUMERLE
  Madam, I know not, nor I greatly care not.
  God knows I had as lief be none as one.
YORK
50 Well, bear you well in this new spring of time,
  Lest you be cropped before you come to prime.
52 What news from Oxford? Do these jousts and tri-
    umphs hold?
AUMERLE
  For aught I know, my lord, they do.
YORK
  You will be there, I know.
AUMERLE
  If God prevent not, I purpose so.
YORK
  What seal is that that hangs without thy bosom?
  Yea, look'st thou pale? Let me see the writing.
AUMERLE
  My lord, 'tis nothing.
YORK   No matter then who see it.
  I will be satisfied; let me see the writing.
AUMERLE
60 I do beseech your grace to pardon me.
  It is a matter of small consequence
  Which for some reasons I would not have seen.
YORK
  Which for some reasons, sir, I mean to see.
  I fear, I fear –
DUCHESS   What should you fear?
65 'Tis nothing but some bond that he is entered into
66 For gay apparel 'gainst the triumph day.
YORK
  Bound to himself? What doth he with a bond
  That he is bound to? Wife, thou art a fool.

---

52 *Do . . . hold* will these tournaments and victory celebrations (at which, according to Holinshed, the conspirators planned to assassinate Richard) be held   **65** *is entered into* has signed   **66** *'gainst* in anticipation of

Boy, let me see the writing.
AUMERLE
I do beseech you pardon me. I may not show it.   *70*
YORK
I will be satisfied. Let me see it, I say.
      He plucks it out of his bosom and reads it.
Treason, foul treason! Villain! traitor! slave!
DUCHESS
What is the matter, my lord?
YORK
Ho! who is within there?
      [Enter a Servant.]   Saddle my horse.
God for his mercy, what treachery is here!   *75*
DUCHESS
Why, what is it, my lord?
YORK
Give me my boots, I say. Saddle my horse.
                              [Exit Servant.]
Now, by mine honor, by my life, by my troth,
I will appeach the villain.   *79*
DUCHESS   What is the matter?
YORK
Peace, foolish woman.   *80*
DUCHESS
I will not peace. What is the matter, Aumerle?
AUMERLE
Good mother, be content. It is no more
Than my poor life must answer.
DUCHESS   Thy life answer?
YORK
Bring me my boots! I will unto the king.
      His Man enters with his boots.
DUCHESS
Strike him, Aumerle. Poor boy, thou art amazed. –   *85*
      [To York's Man]

_____
75 *God . . . mercy* I pray to God for his mercy   79 *appeach* accuse publicly
85 *him* i.e., the servant; *amazed* stunned

Hence, villain! Never more come in my sight.

YORK
Give me my boots, I say!   *[Servant does so and exit.]*

DUCHESS
Why, York, what wilt thou do?
Wilt thou not hide the trespass of thine own?

90 Have we more sons? or are we like to have?
91 Is not my teeming date drunk up with time?
And wilt thou pluck my fair son from mine age
And rob me of a happy mother's name?
Is he not like thee? Is he not thine own?

YORK
Thou fond mad woman,
Wilt thou conceal this dark conspiracy?
A dozen of them here have ta'en the sacrament,
98 And interchangeably set down their hands,
99 To kill the king at Oxford.

DUCHESS   He shall be none;
100 We'll keep him here. Then what is that to him?

YORK
Away, fond woman! Were he twenty times
My son, I would appeach him.

DUCHESS   Hadst thou groaned for
      him
103 As I have done, thou wouldst be more pitiful.
But now I know thy mind. Thou dost suspect
That I have been disloyal to thy bed
And that he is a bastard, not thy son.
Sweet York, sweet husband, be not of that mind!
He is as like thee as a man may be,
Not like to me, or any of my kin,
110 And yet I love him.

YORK   Make way, unruly woman!   *Exit.*

---

91 *teeming date* period of childbearing   **98** *interchangeably . . . hands* signed
reciprocally, so that each had an indenture signed by all   **99** *none* not one of
them   **100** *that* what they do   **103** *pitiful* full of pity

DUCHESS

    After, Aumerle! Mount thee upon his horse,   111

    Spur post and get before him to the king,   112

    And beg thy pardon ere he do accuse thee.

    I'll not be long behind. Though I be old,

    I doubt not but to ride as fast as York;

    And never will I rise up from the ground

    Till Bolingbroke have pardoned thee. Away, be gone!

                                [Exeunt.]

*

❧ **V.3** *Enter the King [Henry IV] with his Nobles [Percy and others].*

KING HENRY

    Can no man tell me of my unthrifty son?   1

    'Tis full three months since I did see him last.

    If any plague hang over us, 'tis he.   3

    I would to God, my lords, he might be found.

    Inquire at London, 'mongst the taverns there,

    For there, they say, he daily doth frequent,

    With unrestrainèd loose companions,   7

    Even such, they say, as stand in narrow lanes

    And beat our watch and rob our passengers,   9

    Whilst he, young wanton and effeminate boy,   10

    Takes on the point of honor to support   11

    So dissolute a crew.

PERCY

    My lord, some two days since I saw the prince

    And told him of those triumphs held at Oxford.

KING HENRY

    And what said the gallant?

---

111 *his horse* one of his horses   112 *Spur post* ride fast

    V.3 Windsor Castle   1 *unthrifty* prodigal   3 *plague* calamity (as prophesied by Carlisle)   7 *loose* wild   9 *watch* night patrolmen; *passengers* travelers   10 *wanton* undisciplined; *effeminate* self-indulgent, voluptuous, weak (as women were imagined to be; see III.2.113 ff.)   11 *Takes on the* takes it as a

PERCY

16   His answer was, he would unto the stews,
And from the common'st creature pluck a glove
And wear it as a favor, and with that
He would unhorse the lustiest challenger.

KING HENRY

20   As dissolute as desperate! Yet through both
I see some sparks of better hope, which elder years
May happily bring forth. But who comes here?
    Enter Aumerle, amazed.

AUMERLE

Where is the king?

KING HENRY

What means our cousin, that he stares and looks
So wildly?

AUMERLE

God save your grace! I do beseech your majesty
To have some conference with your grace alone.

KING HENRY

Withdraw yourselves and leave us here alone.
                 [Exeunt Percy and Lords.]

29   What is the matter with our cousin now?

AUMERLE

30   For ever may my knees grow to the earth,
    [Kneels.]
My tongue cleave to my roof within my mouth,
Unless a pardon ere I rise or speak.

KING HENRY

Intended, or committed, was this fault?

34   If on the first, how heinous e'er it be,
To win thy afterlove I pardon thee.

AUMERLE

Then give me leave that I may turn the key,
That no man enter till my tale be done.

_____

16 *stews* brothels   **20** *desperate* hopeless   **29** *matter* issue, subject of discussion   **34** *on the first* in the first category, intended

KING HENRY

Have thy desire.

[*Aumerle locks the door.*] *The Duke of York knocks at
the door and crieth.*

YORK   *[Within]*

My liege, beware! look to thyself!

Thou hast a traitor in thy presence there.   40

KING HENRY

Villain, I'll make thee safe.

[*Draws his sword.*]

AUMERLE

Stay thy revengeful hand; thou hast no cause to fear.

YORK   *[Within]*

Open the door, secure foolhardy king!   43

Shall I for love speak treason to thy face?   44

Open the door, or I will break it open!

[*Enter York.*]

KING HENRY

What is the matter, uncle? Speak.

Recover breath; tell us how near is danger,

That we may arm us to encounter it.

YORK

Peruse this writing here, and thou shalt know

The treason that my haste forbids me show.   50

AUMERLE

Remember, as thou read'st, thy promise passed.   51

I do repent me. Read not my name there.

My heart is not confederate with my hand.

YORK

It was, villain, ere thy hand did set it down.

I tore it from the traitor's bosom, king.

Fear, and not love, begets his penitence.

Forget to pity him, lest thy pity prove   57

---

43 *secure* overconfident   **44** *speak treason* call you a fool   **50** *haste* breath-
lessness from hurrying   **51** *passed* given, granted   **57** *Forget* forget your
promise

A serpent that will sting thee to the heart.

KING HENRY

59   O heinous, strong, and bold conspiracy!

60   O loyal father of a treacherous son!

61   Thou sheer, immaculate, and silver fountain,
From whence this stream through muddy passages
Hath held his current and defiled himself!

64   Thy overflow of good converts to bad,
And thy abundant goodness shall excuse

66   This deadly blot in thy digressing son.

YORK

67   So shall my virtue be his vice's bawd,
And he shall spend mine honor with his shame,

69   As thriftless sons their scraping fathers' gold.

70   Mine honor lives when his dishonor dies,
Or my shamed life in his dishonor lies.
Thou kill'st me in his life; giving him breath,
The traitor lives, the true man's put to death.

DUCHESS   *[Within]*
What ho, my liege! For God's sake let me in!

KING HENRY
What shrill-voiced suppliant makes this eager cry?

DUCHESS   *[Within]*
A woman, and thy aunt, great king. 'Tis I.
Speak with me, pity me, open the door!
A beggar begs that never begged before.

KING HENRY
Our scene is altered from a serious thing,

80   And now changed to "The Beggar and the King."
My dangerous cousin, let your mother in.
I know she is come to pray for your foul sin.

YORK
If thou do pardon, whosoever pray,

---

59 *strong* flagrant   61 *sheer* pure   64 *converts* changes   66 *digressing* transgressing   67 *bawd* pimp   69 *scraping* saving   80 *"The Beggar . . . King"* (a ballad or jig presumably recounting the story of King Cophetua and the beggarmaid; only the title has relevance here)

More sins for this forgiveness prosper may.
This festered joint cut off, the rest rest sound;
This let alone will all the rest confound.
  [Enter Duchess.]

DUCHESS
  O king, believe not this hardhearted man!
  Love loving not itself, none other can.   88

YORK
  Thou frantic woman, what dost thou make here?   89
  Shall thy old dugs once more a traitor rear?   90

DUCHESS
  Sweet York, be patient. Hear me, gentle liege.
    [Kneels.]

KING HENRY
  Rise up, good aunt.

DUCHESS   Not yet, I thee beseech.
  For ever will I walk upon my knees,
  And never see day that the happy sees,
  Till thou give joy, until thou bid me joy
  By pardoning Rutland, my transgressing boy.

AUMERLE
  Unto my mother's prayers I bend my knee.
    [Kneels.]

YORK
  Against them both my true joints bended be.
    [Kneels.]
  Ill mayst thou thrive if thou grant any grace!

DUCHESS
  Pleads he in earnest? Look upon his face.   *100*
  His eyes do drop no tears, his prayers are in jest;
  His words come from his mouth, ours from our breast.
  He prays but faintly and would be denied;
  We pray with heart and soul and all beside.
  His weary joints would gladly rise, I know;

---

88 *Love . . . can* i.e., if he does not love his own son, he cannot love anyone
else   **89** *make* do   **90** *dugs* breasts; *rear* nurse, breast-feed

106   Our knees still kneel till to the ground they grow.
       His prayers are full of false hypocrisy;
       Ours of true zeal and deep integrity.
       Our prayers do outpray his; then let them have
110   That mercy which true prayer ought to have.

KING HENRY
       Good aunt, stand up.

DUCHESS   Nay, do not say "stand up."
       Say "pardon" first, and afterwards "stand up."
113   An if I were thy nurse, thy tongue to teach,
       "Pardon" should be the first word of thy speech.
       I never longed to hear a word till now.
       Say "pardon," king; let pity teach thee how.
       The word is short, but not so short as sweet;
118   No word like "pardon" for kings' mouths so meet.

YORK
119   Speak it in French, king. Say "Pardonne moy."

DUCHESS
120   Dost thou teach pardon pardon to destroy?
       Ah, my sour husband, my hardhearted lord,
       That sets the word itself against the word!
123   Speak "pardon" as 'tis current in our land;
124   The chopping French we do not understand.
       Thine eye begins to speak, set thy tongue there;
       Or in thy piteous heart plant thou thine ear,
       That hearing how our plaints and prayers do pierce,
128   Pity may move thee "pardon" to rehearse.

KING HENRY
       Good aunt, stand up.

DUCHESS   I do not sue to stand.
130   Pardon is all the suit I have in hand.

KING HENRY
       I pardon him as God shall pardon me.

---

106 *still kneel* will kneel continually   113 *An if* if; *thy tongue . . . teach* who
taught you your first words   118 *meet* suitable   119 *Pardonne moy* i.e., *par-
donnez-moi* ("pardon *me*" in French) – a polite refusal   123 *as . . . land* as
customarily used in English   124 *chopping* (1) broken or choppy, (2) in
which words change their meaning   128 *rehearse* repeat

DUCHESS

    O happy vantage of a kneeling knee!   132

    Yet am I sick for fear. Speak it again.

    Twice saying "pardon" doth not pardon twain,   134

    But makes one pardon strong.

KING HENRY   With all my heart

    I pardon him.

DUCHESS   A god on earth thou art.

    [Rises.]

KING HENRY

    But for our trusty brother-in-law and the abbot,   137

    With all the rest of that consorted crew,   138

    Destruction straight shall dog them at the heels.

    Good uncle, help to order several powers,   *140*

    To Oxford, or where'er these traitors are.

    They shall not live within this world, I swear,

    But I will have them, if I once know where.

    Uncle, farewell; and, cousin, adieu.

    Your mother well hath prayed, and prove you true.

DUCHESS

    Come, my old son. I pray God make thee new.

                            Exeunt.

*

❧ **V.4** *[Enter] Sir Pierce Exton [and Servants].*

EXTON

    Didst thou not mark the king, what words he spake?   1

    "Have I no friend will rid me of this living fear?"

    Was it not so?

MAN   These were his very words.

EXTON

    "Have I no friend?" quoth he. He spake it twice

---

132 *vantage of* (1) advantage of, (2) perspective from   **134** *twain* (1) double,
(2) divide   **137** *brother-in-law* i.e., the Duke of Exeter; *the abbot* (of Westminster)   **138** *consorted crew* conniving gang
  V.4 Windsor Castle   **1** *mark* observe

5   And urged it twice together, did he not?
MAN
     He did.
EXTON
7   And speaking it, he wishtly looked on me,
     As who should say, "I would thou wert the man
     That would divorce this terror from my heart!"
10   Meaning the king at Pomfret. Come, let's go.
11   I am the king's friend, and will rid his foe.   *[Exeunt.]*

                              *

∾ **V.5** *Enter Richard, alone.*

RICHARD
     I have been studying how I may compare
     This prison where I live unto the world;
     And, for because the world is populous,
     And here is not a creature but myself,
     I cannot do it. Yet I'll hammer it out.
     My brain I'll prove the female to my soul,
     My soul the father; and these two beget
8   A generation of still-breeding thoughts;
9   And these same thoughts people this little world,
10   In humors like the people of this world,
     For no thought is contented. The better sort,
     As thoughts of things divine, are intermixed
13   With scruples, and do set the word itself
     Against the word:
15   As thus, "Come, little ones," and then again,
16   "It is as hard to come as for a camel

---

5 *urged . . . together* emphasized it by repeating it   7 *wishtly* intently   **11** *rid* get rid of

V.5 A prison at Pomfret Castle (see note at V.1.52)   **8** *still-breeding* constantly breeding   **9** *little world* i.e., prison cell   **10** *In . . . world* i.e., my thoughts have temperaments just as real people do   **13** *scruples* doubts   **13–14** *set . . . word* find one passage of Scripture that contradicts another   **15** *Come, little ones* (Matthew 19:14, Luke 18:16)   **16–17** *It . . . eye* (Matthew 19:24, Mark 10:25, Luke 18:25)

To thread the postern of a small needle's eye."   17
Thoughts tending to ambition, they do plot   18
Unlikely wonders – how these vain weak nails
May tear a passage through the flinty ribs   20
Of this hard world, my ragged prison walls;   21
And, for they cannot, die in their own pride.   22
Thoughts tending to content flatter themselves
That they are not the first of fortune's slaves,
Nor shall not be the last; like silly beggars   25
Who, sitting in the stocks, refuge their shame,   26
That many have, and others must sit there.
And in this thought they find a kind of ease,
Bearing their own misfortunes on the back
Of such as have before endured the like.   30
Thus play I in one person many people,
And none contented. Sometimes am I king:
Then treasons make me wish myself a beggar,
And so I am. Then crushing penury
Persuades me I was better when a king;
Then am I kinged again; and by and by
Think that I am unkinged by Bolingbroke,
And straight am nothing. But whate'er I be,
Nor I, nor any man that but man is,
With nothing shall be pleased till he be eased   40
With being nothing. *(The music plays.)* Music do I   41
   hear?
Ha – ha – keep time! How sour sweet music is
When time is broke and no proportion kept!   43
So is it in the music of men's lives.
And here have I the daintiness of ear

---

17 *postern* narrow gate   **18** *Thoughts . . . do* my most ambitious thoughts
21 *ragged* rugged   **22** *for* because; *in . . . pride* from their own frustrated ambition   **25** *silly* simple-minded   **26** *the stocks* an engine of punishment in
which the victim's wrists and/or ankles were locked (he or she was then ex-
posed to humiliation and verbal and physical abuse)   **26–27** *refuge . . . That*
find refuge for their shame in the thought that   **41** *being nothing* death   **43**
time rhythm; *broke* disrupted, off; *proportion* harmony

46   To check time broke in a disordered string;
      But, for the concord of my state and time,
48   Had not an ear to hear my true time broke.
      I wasted time, and now doth time waste me;
50   For now hath time made me his numb'ring clock:
51   My thoughts are minutes; and with sighs they jar
52   Their watches on unto mine eyes, the outward watch,
53   Whereto my finger, like a dial's point,
54   Is pointing still, in cleansing them from tears.
55   Now, sir, the sound that tells what hour it is
      Are clamorous groans, which strike upon my heart,
      Which is the bell. so sighs and tears and groans
58   Show minutes, times, and hours. But my time
      Runs posting on in Bolingbroke's proud joy,
60   While I stand fooling here, his Jack of the clock.
61   This music mads me. Let it sound no more;
62   For though it have holp madmen to their wits,
63   In me it seems it will make wise men mad.
      Yet blessing on his heart that gives it me!
      For 'tis a sign of love, and love to Richard
66   Is a strange brooch in this all-hating world.
           Enter a Groom of the stable.

GROOM
67   Hail, royal prince!
RICHARD   Thanks, noble peer.
68   The cheapest of us is ten groats too dear.

---

46 *check* (1) rebuke, (2) detect, hear; *time broke* (1) offbeat time, (2) a wrong note; *disordered* playing ahead of or behind the beat; *string* stringed instrument   48 *time broke* (see 1. 43 gloss)   50 *numbering clock* clock showing hours and minutes (i.e., not an hourglass)   51 *jar* tick 52 *watches* waking periods; *outward watch* clock face (with a play on Richard's *eyes*, sleepless, peering outward)   53 *dial's point* clock hand   54 *still* (1) continually, (2) motionless 55 *Now, sir* (Richard imagines a listener)   58 *times* quarters and halves of the hour   60 *Jack of the clock* mannequin that strikes the hours on an elaborate clock   61 *mads* maddens   62 *holp* helped   63 *wise* sane   66 *strange brooch* rare jewel; *all-hating world* world where I am universally hated   67–68 *royal . . . dear* (two royals or three nobles were worth a pound sterling – the difference between the two coins was ten groats, or fourpence; Richard has been demoted from a *royal* to a *noble*)   68 *cheapest* i.e., Richard

What art thou? and how comest thou hither,
Where no man never comes but that sad dog   70
That brings me food to make misfortune live?

GROOM

I was a poor groom of thy stable, king,
When thou wert king; who, traveling towards York,
With much ado, at length, have gotten leave
To look upon my sometimes royal master's face.
O, how it erned my heart when I beheld,   76
In London streets, that coronation day,
When Bolingbroke rode on roan Barbary,   78
That horse that thou so often hast bestrid,
That horse that I so carefully have dressed!   80

RICHARD

Rode he on Barbary? Tell me, gentle friend,
How went he under him?

GROOM

So proudly as if he disdained the ground.

RICHARD

So proud that Bolingbroke was on his back!
That jade hath eat bread from my royal hand;   85
This hand hath made him proud with clapping him.   86
Would he not stumble? would he not fall down,
Since pride must have a fall, and break the neck
Of that proud man that did usurp his back?
Forgiveness, horse! Why do I rail on thee,   90
Since thou, created to be awed by man,
Wast born to bear? I was not made a horse;
And yet I bear a burden like an ass,
Spurred, galled, and tired by jauncing Bolingbroke.   94
        Enter one [Keeper] to Richard with meat.

KEEPER

Fellow, give place. Here is no longer stay.   95

---

70 *no . . . never* (an emphatic double negative); *sad dog* dismal fellow **76**
erned my heart caused my heart to mourn **78** *roan* of mottled color; *Barbary*
(the horse's name) **80** *dressed* groomed **85** *eat* eaten **86** *with clapping* by
petting **94** *jauncing* making the horse prance, riding showily **95** *give place*
leave

RICHARD

If thou love me, 'tis time thou wert away.

GROOM

What my tongue dares not, that my heart shall say.

Exit Groom.

KEEPER

My lord, will't please you to fall to?

RICHARD

99   Taste of it first, as thou art wont to do.

KEEPER

100   My lord, I dare not. Sir Pierce of Exton,

Who lately came from the king, commands the contrary.

RICHARD

The devil take Henry of Lancaster, and thee!

Patience is stale, and I am weary of it.

[Beats the Keeper.]

KEEPER

Help, help, help!

The Murderers [Exton and Servants] rush in.

RICHARD

How now! What means death in this rude assault?

Villain, thy own hand yields thy death's instrument.

[Snatches a weapon from a Servant and kills him.]

107   Go thou and fill another room in hell.

[Kills another.] Here Exton strikes him down.

That hand shall burn in never-quenching fire

109   That staggers thus my person. Exton, thy fierce hand

110   Hath with the king's blood stained the king's own land.

Mount, mount, my soul! thy seat is up on high;

Whilst my gross flesh sinks downward, here to die.

[Dies.]

EXTON

As full of valor as of royal blood!

Both have I spilled. O, would the deed were good!

---

99 *Taste . . . first* (a taster to insure that food was not poisoned was a royal prerogative)   **107** *room* place   **109** *staggers* makes stagger

For now the devil, that told me I did well,
Says that this deed is chronicled in hell.
This dead king to the living king I'll bear.
Take hence the rest, and give them burial here.

                                              [Exeunt.]

                        *

‧‧ **V.6** *[Flourish.] Enter Bolingbroke [as King], with the
Duke of York [, other Lords, and Attendants].*

KING
    Kind uncle York, the latest news we hear
    Is that the rebels have consumed with fire
    Our town of Ciceter in Gloucestershire;   3
    But whether they be ta'en or slain we hear not.
      Enter Northumberland.
    Welcome, my lord. What is the news?
NORTHUMBERLAND
    First, to thy sacred state wish I all happiness.
    The next news is, I have to London sent
    The heads of Salisbury, Spencer, Blunt, and Kent.
    The manner of their taking may appear   9
    At large discoursèd in this paper here.   10
KING
    We thank thee, gentle Percy, for thy pains
    And to thy worth will add right worthy gains.
      Enter Lord Fitzwater.
FITZWATER
    My lord, I have from Oxford sent to London
    The heads of Brocas and Sir Bennet Seely,
    Two of the dangerous consorted traitors
    That sought at Oxford thy dire overthrow.
KING
    Thy pains, Fitzwater, shall not be forgot.
    Right noble is thy merit, well I wot.
      Enter Henry Percy [and the Bishop of Carlisle].

―――――
V.6 Windsor Castle   **3** *Ciceter* i.e., Cirencester   **9** *taking* capture

PERCY
       The grand conspirator, Abbot of Westminster,
20   With clog of conscience and sour melancholy
       Hath yielded up his body to the grave;
22   But here is Carlisle living, to abide
23   Thy kingly doom and sentence of his pride.
KING
       Carlisle, this is your doom:
25   Choose out some secret place, some reverend room,
26   More than thou hast, and with it joy thy life.
       So, as thou liv'st in peace, die free from strife;
       For though mine enemy thou hast ever been,
       High sparks of honor in thee have I seen.
              Enter Exton, with [Attendants bearing] the coffin.
EXTON
30   Great king, within this coffin I present
       Thy buried fear. Herein all breathless lies
       The mightiest of thy greatest enemies,
       Richard of Bordeaux, by me hither brought.
KING
       Exton, I thank thee not; for thou hast wrought
35   A deed of slander, with thy fatal hand,
       Upon my head and all this famous land.
EXTON
       From your own mouth, my lord, did I this deed.
KING
       They love not poison that do poison need,
       Nor do I thee. Though I did wish him dead,
40   I hate the murderer, love him murder'ed.
       The guilt of conscience take thou for thy labor,
       But neither my good word nor princely favor.
43   With Cain go wander through shades of night,
       And never show thy head by day nor light.

---

20 *With clog* under the crippling weight   **22** *abide* await   **23** *doom* (l) judgment, (2) punishment, (3) fate   **25** *reverend room* place of religious retirement   **26** *joy* enjoy   **35** *deed of slander* deed to rouse slanderous talk against the crown   **43** *Cain* (who slew his brother Abel; see I.1.104 and Genesis 4:12, 14)